T0328364

ESSAYS ON SELECTED CONTEMPORARY ISSUES IN THE NIGERIAN BANKING SYSTEM

ESSAYS ON SELECTED CONTEMPORARY ISSUES IN THE NIGERIAN BANKING SYSTEM

UMARU IBRAHIM, FCIB, mni
Managing Director/Chief Executive Officer
Nigeria Deposit Insurance Corporation
(2010-2020)

Safari Books Ltd
Ibadan

Published by
Safari Books Ltd
Ile Ori Detu
1, Shell Close
Onireke
Ibadan.
Email: safarinigeria@gmail.com
Website: http://safaribooks.com.ng

© 2021, Umaru Ibrahim FCIB, mni
First Published 2021

All rights reserved. This book is copyright and so no part of it may be reproduced, stored in a retrieval system, or transmitted, in any form or by any means, electrical, mechanical, electrostatic, magnetic tape, photocopying, recording or otherwise, without the prior written permission of the author.

ISBN: 978-978-58008-4-5 Cased
978-978-58008-5-2 Paperback

CONTENTS

PREVIEW OF CHAPTERS

The relevance of Deposit Insurance System (DIS) in financial system stability globally is becoming more prominent, the reason for which increasing number of countries are setting up deposit insurance system, while some others are changing the types and structures of existing DIS. The rapid rise in technological innovation pose new challenges for DIS in developing countries, especially Nigeria, characterised by poor or very low public awareness of the existence of the DIS and its operations. The asymmetry between the complexity in financial systems development and public awareness of the DIS, against the background of Nigeria's ambition to be the financial hub of West Africa by 2020, is at the heart of the compilation of this book. The book focuses on the Deposit Insurance experience in Nigeria, with experience drawn from other comparator countries, its evolution and relation with the financial sector.

Chapter One describes the 'Risk Management: Global Emerging Trends.' Risk management in the banking sector, the 2007/09 Global Financial Crisis (GFC) and its impact on the Nigerian banking sector are discussed. Lessons from the GFC are presented.

Chapter Two discusses the 'Role of Microfinance Banks in Economic Development', outlining the objectives of the microfinance, the licensing requirements, the dynamic linkage between microfinance and rural development, the prospect for microfinance growth and the role of the NDIC in repositioning microfinance banks in Nigeria.

Chapter Three explores the contemporary issues around the mobile payment services and its integrity in Nigeria, as a potent instrument to spur financial inclusion to meet the 80% target in 2020.

Chapter Four handles the narratives around the role of Deposit Insurance in promoting financial inclusion and poverty alleviation as well as the role of the NDIC in driving financial inclusion in Nigeria.

Chapter Five discusses deposit insurance and consumer protection arrangement in Nigeria and the role of and challenges faced by the NDIC in enhancing consumer protection.

Chapter Six focuses on the strategies for addressing customer complaints in the banking system. The challenges and prospects of handling customer complaints through the regulatory framework are presented.

Chapter Seven is on emerging issues in corporate governance. It emphasises the need for directors, regulators, shareholders, policy-makers to pay greater attention to the issue of corporate governance in their organisations and highlights the legislations guiding the responsibilities and liabilities of directors in organisations.

Chapter Eight discusses the potential stimulating role of corporate social responsibility in poverty reduction and economic development, the core principles of corporate social responsibility and the convergence of corporate social responsibility with corporate governance are discussed. The experience of the NDIC in this context are highlighted.

Chapter Nine explains the official safety-nets and stakeholders' protection during banking crisis and examines the role of deposit insurance within the nation's safety nets and the regulatory response to financial crisis by the NDIC as a risk minimiser.

Chapter Ten on 'Financial System Resilience in a Globalised Economy: Prospects, Threats and Benefits to the Nigerian Financial Sector', stresses the interconnectedness in today's global financial systems and highlights the role of the NDIC in achieving financial system stability in Nigeria.

Chapter Eleven examines 'Bank Failure Resolution Measures: Nigerian Experience'. The crucial role played by banks as the financial intermediary between the deficit and surplus economic units, the risks of exposure and the available resolution options for bank failures are discussed. The IADI core principles as they relate to failure resolution and their nexus with Financial Safety Board (FSB) key attributes are presented.

Chapter Twelve presents the building blocks to sustainable banking practice in Nigeria. It explains the concept and practice of sustainable banking in Nigeria and elaborates on the initiatives of the NDIC and CBN in promoting sustainable banking.

LIST OF ABBREVIATIONS AND ACRONYMS

AFI	-	Alliance for Financial Inclusion
AMCON	-	Asset Management Corporation of Nigeria
AMPI	-	African Mobile Phone Financial Services Policy Initiative
ASI	-	Nigerian Stock Exchange All-Share Index
ATM	-	Automated Teller Machine
BCBS	-	Basel Committee on Banking Supervision
BOFIA	-	Banks and Other Financial Institutions Act
BSI	–	British Standards Institution
CAMA	-	Companies and Allied Matters Act
CBN	–	Central Bank of Nigeria
CD	–	Certificate of Deposit
CG	–	Corporate Governance
CIBN	-	Chartered Institute of Bankers of Nigeria
CIDA	-	Canadian International Development Agency
CIPD	–	Chartered Institute of Personnel and Development
CIPM	–	Chartered Institute of Personnel Management of Nigeria
CMF	-	Committee on Financial Markets
CMGs	-	Crisis Management Groups
CP	–	Commercial Paper
CSR	-	Corporate Social Responsibility

DFID	-	Department for International Development
DFIs	-	Development Finance Institutions
DIF	-	Deposit Insurance Fund
DIS	-	Deposit Insurance Systems
DMBs	-	Deposit Money Banks
DPAS	-	Differential Premium Assessment System
D-SIBs	-	Domestic Systemically Important Banks
eFASS	-	Electronic Financial Analysis Surveillance System
EFInA	-	Enhancing Financial Innovation and Access
ESRM	-	Environmental and Social Risk Management
FCT	-	Federal Capital Territory
FIs	-	Financial institutions
FDI	–	Foreign Direct Investment
FMF	–	Federal Ministry of Finance
FRC	-	Financial Reporting Council
FSB	-	Financial Standard Board
FSF	-	Financial Stability Fund
FSRCC	-	Financial Services Regulation Coordinating Committee
G-SIFIs	-	Global Systemically Important Financial Institutions
HOLDCO	-	Holding Companies
IADI	-	International Association of Deposit Insurers
IFC	-	International Finance Corporation
ILO	-	International Labour Organisation
INSEAD	-	Institut Européen d'Administration des Affaires

IoD	–	Institute of Directors
KYC	-	Know Your Customer
LOLR	-	Lender of last resort
M & A	-	Mergers and Acquisition
MCP	-	Microfinance Certification Programme
MDGs	-	Millennium Development Goals
MFBs	-	Microfinance Banks
MFIs	-	Microfinance Institutions
MFS	-	Mobile Financial Services
MMO	-	Mobile Money Operators
MoU	–	Memorandum of Understanding
M-Pesa	–	Mobile Payments (Swahili)
MSME	-	Micro, Small and Medium Enterprises
MSMEDF	-	Micro, Small and Medium-Scale Enterprises Development Fund
NCC	-	Nigerian Communications Commission
NDIC	-	Nigeria Deposit Insurance Corporation
NEDs	-	Non-Executive Directors
NEEDS	-	National Economic Empowerment and Development Strategy
NFC	-	Near Field Communication
NFIS	-	National Financial Inclusion Strategy
NIBSS	-	Nigerian Interbank Settlement System
NIM	–	Nigerian Institute of Management
NIPSS	–	National Institute for Policy and Strategic Studies
NPL	-	Non-Performing Loan
NSBP	-	Nigeria Sustainable Banking Principles
OBA	-	Open Bank Assistance
ODA	-	Official Development Assistance
OECD	-	Organisation for Economic Co-operation and Development
RTGS	-	Real-Time Gross Settlement

PFIs	-	Participating Financial Institutions
P&A	-	Purchase and Assumption
PMBs	-	Primary Mortgage Banks
POS	–	Point of Sale
PTDI	-	Pass-through Deposit Insurance
SBN	-	Sustainable Banking Network
SDGs	-	Sustainable Development Goals
SEMOPS	-	Secured Mobile Payment System
SPVs	-	Special Purpose Vehicles
SSWG	-	Strategic Sustainable Workgroup
USSD	-	Unstructured Supplementary Service Data

FOREWORD

The Nigeria Deposit Insurance Corporation (NDIC), established by Decree No. 22 of 1988, was repealed and re-enacted as the NDIC Act No. 16 of 2006. The Corporation commenced operations in March 1989. Through its activities, the NDIC has effectively brought to the fore the need to strengthen and broaden financial safety-nets, especially the aspect of deposit insurance, aimed at safeguarding depositors' funds, during periods of financial distress. The objectives of the safety-net include: protecting consumers of financial services, especially depositors; ensuring the stability and integrity of the financial system, by encouraging prudent risk-taking; promoting competition and efficiency in the financial sector, by reducing competitive barriers in the deposit-taking industry and ensuring orderly resolution of failing and failed financial institutions.

This book *Essays on Selected Contemporary Issues in the Nigerian Banking System,* explores a number of conceptual and emerging issues in deposit insurance, the mobile payments system, corporate governance, bank failure resolution options, and some narratives around financial crisis viz-a-viz deposit insurance. The issues discussed are not only relevant, but also fundamental to financial system stability. The author's knowledge and practical experience in the nation's financial services industry, spanning over three decades and his active participation in policy design/implementation, were effectively brought to bear in this compendium of articles on deposit insurance, finance and economic issues. This book thus covers topical issues on risk management, failure resolution measures, the role of deposit insurance during banking crisis, the importance of deposit insurance in consumer protection and financial system resilience.

The author, Umaru Ibrahim, FCIB, mni, graduated from the Ahmadu Bello University, Zaria, Nigeria, in 1974. In 1977, he obtained a Master of Public Administration (M.P.A) from the same university. In 2001, he attended the prestigious National Institute for Policy and Strategic Studies (NIPSS), Kuru, where he bagged 'the member of the National Institute' (mni). In furtherance of his practical knowledge, Ibrahim attended several technical and management courses at a number of prestigious institutions both locally and abroad. These institutions include the ESSEC Graduate Business School, France; Templeton College of Oxford University, U.K.; and International Centre for Banking and Financial Services, Manchester University. Others are the Royal Institute of Public Administration, London; the International Institute for Management Development (IMD), Lausanne, Switzerland; INSEAD France; and ROSS School of Business, University of Michigan, USA.

Ibrahim had an enviable work experience. He joined the Kano State Public Service in 1975, after the one-year compulsory National Service in Rivers State. While in Kano, he diligently served in several Ministries and Departments, rising to the post of Permanent Secretary in 1984, a position he held till 1989. He joined the NDIC in May 1989 as a Deputy Director, and Head, Financial and Technical Support, one of the key operational departments of NDIC then. He became a Director in charge of the Administration Department of NDIC in 1991. Between 1992 and 2007, he headed several other departments, including the Human Resources Department. In August 2007, Ibrahim was appointed the Executive Director of the NDIC in charge of Corporate Services. In December 2009, he was appointed Acting Managing Director/ Chief Executive Officer of the Corporation. On the 8th of December 2010, he was appointed as the substantive Managing Director/Chief Executive Officer of the NDIC for an initial term of five years; he was reappointed for a second term of five years in December 2015.

Under Ibrahim's leadership, the NDIC met the stringent requirements for certification by the British Standard Institution (BSI) in three areas: ISO 27001:2013 (Information Security Management); ISO 22301:2012 (Business Continuity Management); and ISO 20000:2011 (IT Service Management). In recognition of the tremendous performance of the NDIC at the local and international levels, Ibrahim was elected in 2013 as an Executive Council (EXCO) member of the International Association of Deposit Insurers (IADI) based in Basel, Switzerland. IADI is a forum for deposit insurers from around the world to share their experiences and benefit from one another in the field of deposit insurance. Ibrahim is also a member of the Board of Assets Management Corporation of Nigeria (AMCON), the Governing Board of the FITC and the Fellows Selection Committee of the Chartered Institute of Bankers of Nigeria (CIBN).

He is a member/fellow of several professional bodies, including: Fellow, Nigerian Institute of Management (NIM); Fellow, Society for Corporate Governance of Nigeria; Fellow, CIBN; Fellow Institute of Directors

(IoD) Nigeria; Member, Chartered Institute of Personnel Management (CIPM); Member, Alumni Association of the National Institute for Policy and Strategic Studies (NIPSS); and Certified International Director (INSEAD CIDP).

In this book, Umaru Ibrahim brings to bear his considerable experience in discussing a number of key issues in the Nigeria financial system in a lucid way that makes for an engaging reading that will appeal not only to professionals, but anyone seeking practical knowledge in the regulation of the financial systems, especially in Nigeria.

I recommend the book to the general reader, the classroom lecturer and the professional in the banking system.

Mrs Zainab Shamsuna Ahmed
Minister, Federal Ministry of Finance,
Budget and National Planning
August 2020

PREFACE

The relative dearth of literature, particularly on deposit insurance in both Nigeria and other African countries, was the impetus for bringing together in a book form, papers and speeches I presented on contemporary issues in the Nigerian financial system. The topics cover the burning issues of deposit insurance, banking crisis dynamics, corporate governance, mobile payment services and consumer protection. Developments in the areas covered by this book of readings will continue to impact operations and practices in the field of banking and finance in Nigeria. Having shared these thoughts with the public through incisive presentations/speeches at various fora within and outside Nigeria, it became expedient to put together these papers and speeches in a book form for wider readership and appreciation. The book provides the opportunity for me to propagate the core mandate of the NDIC to the general public and hence raise the public awareness about the Deposit Insurance System (DIS) in Nigeria, which we consider relatively low even among the educated elite. It is also my ardent belief that the book will add to extant literature, particularly in the area of deposit insurance, bank failure resolution and other topical issues. I am, therefore, convinced that the book will become a necessary and reliable handbook for budding students, researchers and practitioners in finance and banking both in Nigeria and among members of the IADI.

I want to thank the former Director, NDIC Research Department, Dr. J. G. Donli for his role in carefully selecting the articles from the retinue of speeches I delivered at various fora and arranging them in an order that will make an interesting reading. I also earnestly appreciate the efforts of the NDIC research team headed by S. A. Oluyemi, Director, Research Department, in fine-tuning the articles and updating the information and statistics to reflect current developments in the industry. Other members of the NDIC research team to whom I owe gratitude include, K. O. Nwaigwe (Deputy Director), H. I. Ahmad (Deputy Director), K. S. Katata (Deputy Director) and A. Abdulrasheed (Principal Manager), all in the Research Department of the NDIC. I also want to thank the secretariat and other staff of the NDIC too numerous to mention.

Finally, a successful completion of a book project of this nature rests solely on measured level of comfort provided by some spirited family members. On this, I want to thank every member of my immediate family for their support and understanding throughout the duration of the book project.

Umaru Ibrahim, FCIB, mni
Managing Director/Chief Executive Officer
Nigeria Deposit Insurance Corporation
August 2020

1

RISK MANAGEMENT: GLOBAL EMERGING
TRENDS[1]

1.0   Introduction

The change and expansion of financial services over time underscores the importance of knowing how to measure and manage the risks associated with new business practices. A consequence of this change has been an increase in the exposure of financial markets to risks. This risk exposure due to changing business activities and environment could be catastrophic for individual financial systems as well as have a contagion effect if these risks are not managed properly. Thus, an organisation must study, understand and define its risk management strategy to ensure proper management of risk and also improve overall business performance. Risk management can come in various forms including

---

1   Original version of the keynote address was delivered at 2012 Risk Management Association Conference, Lagos

accepting the risk and developing strategies to minimise its negative impact, limiting exposure to risk and avoiding risk all together. Limiting exposure to risk and risk avoidance may seem rational, however, evading risk may deny an organisation operational benefits that come with accepting and managing such risk (Audu, 2014).

This chapter discusses risk management in the banking industry. Section 1.2 briefly examines risk and risk management in banking. Section 1.3 discusses types of financial crisis while section 1.4 reviews the global financial crisis of 2007-09. Section 1.5 presents the impact of the global financial crisis on the Nigerian banking system and economy. In section 1.6, lessons from the global financial crisis are presented and section 1.7 concludes the chapter.

1.2   Risk Management

Risk can be defined as the likelihood of occurrence of an unwanted event capable of damaging an asset and possibly result in financial loss (Audu, 2014). Risk is caused by external or internal elements and may be avoided through pre-emptive action. Risk is associated with uncertainty and is an essential part of business because businesses grow by taking risk. Risk and risk management cut across all sectors of the economy, especially banking.

Audu (2014) categorised risk into two main groups: Systemic (Non-Diversifiable) and Un-systemic (Diversifiable) risks. The Systemic/Non-diversifiable risk is also referred to as undiversified or market risk. It cannot be eliminated or avoided by diversification but can be alleviated through hedging. Systemic risk, like interest rate, is macro by nature affecting several firms and influences several assets.

The other risk type is the unsystemic risk, sometimes referred to as "specific risk" or diversified risk. Being diversifiable, the risk can be eliminated by diversification and is micro in nature as it affects only a particular organisation and not the whole system. Examples of this category of risk are operational risk, business risk, financial risk and liquidity risk.

For Global Association of Risk Professionals, GARP (2009), the risks faced by all businesses can be grouped into the following five broad categories: market, credit or default, operational, liquidity and political or regulatory risks. Market, credit and operational are categorised as the main and quantifiable risks to an entity. There can be significant economic consequences if any type is not well managed.

Market risk refers to the risk of loss emanating from the wrong valuation of asset prices due to the adverse movements in market prices. Credit risk occurs when a debtor defaults on a loan or other line of credit and from a change in the credit quality of a counterparty resulting from a market-base revaluation; probably due to a rating agency downgrade, or from actual default. Credit risk happens to be the largest component of risk in the banking sector. Operational risk could result from insufficient or failed systems, processes, and people as well as from external developments.

Risk management is the identification, assessment, and prioritisation of risks, as well as a coordinated use of resources to monitor and control its negative impact (Audu, 2014). Risk management can also be defined as the use of techniques to reduce the possibility of occurrence of negative events without incurring excessive costs and hampering the operations of an enterprise. In other words, risk management involves identifying and understanding key risks and developing processes to monitor and control their effect. Figure 1.1 shows a simplified risk management process.

Figure 1.1: Simplified risk management process

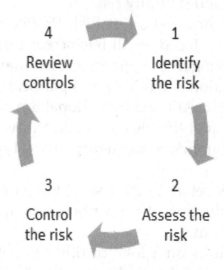

Source: Adopted from www.corporatefinanceinstitute.com.

Risk management does not eliminate risks but manage them instead, in order to exploit opportunities and reduce threats. Good risk management entails a proactive rather than reactive control of future outcomes. In addition to predicting the effect of risk on a business, a good risk management strategy should also calculate the uncertainties associated with risks. By engaging in risk management, prospective problems can be detected before they materialise, and an enterprise-wide risk management strategy can be developed and implemented to manage the risks. Risk management helps to:

(i)   Identify risk elements inherent in a given system.

(ii)   Prevent undue exposure to both internal (events within an organisation), or external (events in the wider business arena) risk elements that can undermine the operations of a given system.

(iii)   Prevent systemic failure by providing early warning signals on any threat.

(iv)   Access the effectiveness of risk management strategies already deployed to mitigate identified risks.

(v)   Improve decision making by providing management with the nature of risks that may impede the organisation's overall strategies and objectives.

(vi)   Develop effective strategies to manage performance and accountability.

1.3   Financial Crisis

Financial crisis has a complicated relationship with risk management. According to Claessens & Kose (2013), financial crises are extreme expressions of the connections between the financial sector and the real economy and require an understanding of macrofinancial linkages. The authors broadly classified them into four types: Currency, Sudden stop, Foreign & Domestic Debt Crises as well as Banking Crises.

Currency crisis comprises a speculative attack on a nation's currency that leads to devaluation or compel the authorities to defend the currency through huge spending of its foreign reserves, or sharply raising interest rates, or establishing capital controls. Theories on currency crises have evolved over time, in part due to their changing nature. Particularly, the literature has evolved from focusing on the key causes of currency crises to discussing the scope for multiple equilibria and to emphasising the role financial variables such as changes in balance sheets, play in triggering the crises.

In the last four decades, three generations of models have been typically used to explain currency crises. The first generation of models was motivated to a large extent by the collapse in the price of gold. The second generation of models emphasise the importance of multiple equilibria. Second generation models show that uncertainty on the willingness of a government to maintain its exchange rate peg could lead to multiple equilibria and currency crises. Prediction is possible with these models. The third generation models show how deteriorations of bank balance sheets due to fluctuations in asset prices and exchange rates can lead to currency crises. Third generation models were largely motivated by the Asian crises of the late 90s.

For a sudden stop (or a capital account or balance of payments crisis), this crisis arises when a big (and often unanticipated) reduction in international capital inflows or a sharp reversal in cumulative capital flows to a country happens. It may probably occur together with a sharp growth in its credit spreads. Sudden stop models tend to give greater significance to the role of international factors such as changes in international interest rates in causing 'sudden stops' in capital flows. These models do not explain properly, the sharp drops in output and Total Factor Productivity. However, they can account for the current account reversals and the depreciation in real exchange rate observed during crises in emerging markets.

A foreign debt crisis occurs when a nation becomes unable to or refuses to service its foreign debt. It can be either sovereign or private (or both) debt crisis. As the name denotes, domestic public debt crisis is the crisis that occurs when a nation fails to honour its debt obligation in one form or the other. Theories on foreign debt crises and default are closely linked to those explaining sovereign lending. Models on foreign debt crises are designed as gross simplification on either intratemporal or intertemporal sanction. Intertemporal sanctions arise from threat of cut-off from future lending if a country defaults. Intratemporal sanctions arise from the inability to earn foreign exchange due to imposition of sanctions by trading partners. Such sanctions may be in the form of denying the country access to the international market for some time.

Systemic banking crisis occur due to actual or probable bank runs and failures can make banks to interrupt the convertibility of their liabilities or force the government to intervene by rendering assistance on a large scale. Banking crises are quite common and may also be the least understood type of crises. The fragility of banks makes them subject to runs by depositors and the problems in one bank can quickly spread to other banks, leading to a contagion effect. Public safety nets inclusive of deposit insurance can limit this risk, albeit, this support comes with distortions that may increase the likelihood of a crisis. A second factor that can increase the risk of bank crises is institutional weakness. Because banks heavily depend on legal, judicial and information environments to make prudent investment decisions and collect their loans, with institutional weaknesses, the risk of a banking crisis can be higher. Over the centuries, several banking crises have occurred, displaying some common patterns which have been identified.

1.4 Global Financial Crises (2007-2009)

The term financial meltdown defines moments when financial networks and markets suddenly become markedly unstable or strained to the point where they may collapse. It features sudden change in expectations, speculative bubbles, falling prices and frequent bankruptcies. From 2002 to early 2007, market risks lowered due to the reduction in volatility of global financial markets. This period was characterised by a huge increase in subprime mortgage lending in the USA. Sub-prime mortgages are mortgages that are considered to be significantly riskier than average. Eventually, this led to more foreclosures, a further increase in the supply of houses for sale, and a further decline in house prices. As foreclosures increased, the losses on mortgages also increased.

From 2007, the United States experienced the worst financial crisis since the 1930s, that quickly spread rapidly to other nations and from the banking system to the real economy. Some financial institutions failed while many had to be bailed out by governments.

Various factors have been attributed to the origin of the sub-prime crises (Sanusi, 2010). These include:

(i) Low real interests rates in the US. This interest was maintained for a long time prior to the crises and this encouraged accommodating monetary policies.

(ii) High confidence in the continued rise of house prices and low volatility in the US housing market.

(iii) A shift in the mortgage lending policy to less credit worthy borrowers, marginal borrowers and sub-prime borrowers who did not qualify for prime mortgage. Furthermore, in the sub-prime market, more than 50% of the loans were made by independent mortgage brokers who were not supervised at the federal level unlike banks.

(iv) Incentive problem for independent credit rating agencies who were involved in developing structured products they rated and incentive problems associated with securitisation models for mortgage loans into mortgage backed securities.

The sub-prime crises actually started in 2007, however, its effect was not dramatic at the time as affected investment banks wrote down their losses hence, eroding their capital. The realised losses increased substantially when the contagion spread to other counterparties that invested heavily in structured products. The contagion assumed a global scale because the investors were not only US companies. This became a contagion around the globe.

As at August 2007, financial institutions in the United States were experiencing liquidity constraints and by March 2008, there was a credit crunch. During that time, defaults in many markets were widespread and by July 2008, defaults were reported in other economies. By the last quarter of 2008, European countries and the US officially declared that they were in economic recession. As a consequence, the resulting distortions to national economies became unprecedented.

1.5 Impact of the Global Financial Crises (GFC) on the Nigerian Economy and Nigerian Banking Sector (Sanusi, 2010)

1.5.1. Impact on the Nigerian Economy

In Nigeria, the initial impact of the crises was not felt due to sound macroeconomic policies and also, the Nigerian banking system was less integrated with the global financial market. Furthermore, the banking system had strong capitalisation due to the recapitalisation exercise of 2005. However, as the recession in the advanced countries deepened, the Nigerian economy and financial sector became affected.

The GFC manifested itself in the form of liquidity and credit crunch, weak consumer demand, lack of confidence in the banking system, inability of banks to improve capital adequacy ratio, de-leveraging of banks and a fall in the global output. Nigeria was not insulated from the GFC as it was affected in the financial and real sectors.

Nigeria's undiversified economy, high dependence on foreign exchange earnings from crude oil and high dependence on export of crude oil exacerbated the impact from the financial crises as Nigeria experienced low demand for its oil due to recession in the economies of her trading partners. The low foreign exchange reserves as well as pressure on foreign exchange due to demand led to depreciation in the naira exchange rate. To finance its activities, government resorted to withdrawals from the Excess Crude Account and domestic borrowing.

1.5.2. Impact on the Nigerian Banking Sector

In mid-2008 when the GFC set in, several interdependent factors at play in the domestic financial system led to the re-emergence of an extremely fragile financial system similar to pre-consolidation era. These factors included significant failures in corporate governance at banks, macroeconomic instability caused by large and sudden capital inflows, low level of investor and consumer sophistication, weak business environment and weak governing and management processes at the CBN.

These weaknesses meant that when the GFC eventually hit Nigeria, the banking sector was not equipped to weather the storm in spite of the recapitalisation. This resulted in a sharp deterioration in the quality of banks' assets which immediately led to concerns over banks' liquidity. As a result, the Nigerian banking sector was thrown into major crisis as many of the banks became distressed.

1.5.3. Key Reforms in the Nigerian Banking Sector

The CBN in June 2009, took a three-pronged approach to assess the financial condition of the 24 DMBs. The first was a special examination exercise jointly carried out by the CBN and the NDIC. That exercise highlighted weaknesses in risk management practices and corporate governance, as well as inadequacies in liquidity ratios and capital asset ratios in 9 banks. These banks failed to meet the minimum 10% capital adequacy ratio and 25 per cent minimum liquidity ratio. Apart from accumulating a large number of non-performing loans, these banks were seriously exposed to the oil and gas sector as well as the capital market. The report of the audit exercise revealed greater magnitude of weak financial condition of the nine banks as all of them were "technically" insolvent with significant negative asset values.

Against this backdrop, the CBN moved to strengthen the industry, protect depositors and creditors, restore public confidence and safeguard the integrity of the Nigerian banking industry. Initial measures/initiatives taken by the CBN in conjunction with NDIC and the Federal Ministry of Finance included: injection of ₦620 billion into the nine banks; the replacement of the chief executive/executive directors of eight of the nine banks with competent managers; and guaranteeing foreign creditors and correspondent banks' credit lines in order to restore confidence and maintain important correspondent banking relationships.

The third approach was to carry out management account audit of the affected banks by their new management. The outcome was very much in line with that of the audit report. Consequently, a number of actions were taken by the management under the guidance of the CBN to ensure that the banks operated effectively with particular emphasis on improving transparency and operations.

In addition to the CBN's three-pronged approach, long term reforms measures were adopted by the CBN, in four areas, namely:

- Enhancing the quality of banks;
- Establishment of financial stability;
- Enabling healthy financial sector evolution; and
- Ensuring the financial sector contributes to the real economy.

1.6 Lessons from the Global Financial Crises

Following the Global Financial Crises, a number of lessons have been learned.

(i) Pre-crisis risk analysis often assumed that the near future would resemble the near past. However, this assumption was a mistake as the global economy painfully experienced. The use of such limited bases for assessing risk and not taking into account extreme scenarios caused many financial firms to take large risk positions that seemed safe and adequate. The recent crises showed that these had led to gross underestimation of risks in most situations. In response, modern risk management is focused on model sophistication in estimating probabilities of extreme losses and rare events as well as stress testing.

(ii) The crises led to an increased focus on and monitoring of systemic risk by regulators. A naive assessment of risk management procedures might indicate that the overall financial system is well-hedged if individual financial institutions are well-hedged. However, the 2007-2009 experience strongly suggests that individual stability of firms is quite different from systemic stability. This is because risk can spread from one bank to another through the interconnections between banks. It can also do so because banks operate in a common economic and regulatory environment and are thus exposed to common factors.

(iii) More attention is paid to counterparty risk. The collapse of AIG and the failures of Bear Stearns and Lehman Brothers in the USA were reminders that high credit ratings cannot substitute for due diligence and careful monitoring of counterparties. The financial crisis has therefore accelerated a trend that started earlier to substantially improve the management of counterparty risk.

(iv) The identification of credit ratings as a factor that contributed significantly to the global financial crises has reduced reliance on credit ratings. As an alternative, market participants are required to significantly improve their credit analysis.

(v) Mispricing of assets due to the use of models that relied heavily on inputs from credit ratings has led to an increased consideration of model risk.

(vi) Presently, increased attention is given to sovereign risk. The European crises, recent US downgrade and risks posed by political decisions that can have a global effect have made sovereign risk management a global trend as opposed to an emerging market trend.

(vii) There is the introduction of new regulatory rules worldwide. In the midst of the crisis, Basel II.V (2.5) was quickly instituted to deal with the shortcomings of Basel II. New regulatory requirements in the name of Basel III will be phased-in gradually. Also, the US government introduced the Dodd-Frank Act and a wide range of regulatory changes.

(viii) The credit crisis has led to a new focus on funding liquidity. The realisations that liquidity or lack of liquidity contributed significantly to the failure of financial institutions has made regulators in many countries attach increased significance to liquidity management. The result is a closer supervision of liquidity as seen in the proposed liquidity buffers for banks as part of Basel III.

(ix) Another major trend is rising derivatives usage with associated tighter regulation. What's really scary however is not the size of derivatives turnover but how complex and unregulated derivatives instruments are. It is a fact that other derivatives can be used for hedging, speculation or arbitrage. And it is not easy to know for which reason the derivative is being used by a firm. Regulators will therefore require greater disclosure towards derivatives transactions.

(x) A new important trend is the rising use of contingent convertibles, also known as CoCo bonds or CoCos by banks. CoCos are different from regular convertible bonds in that the likelihood of the bonds converting to equity is "contingent" on a specified event.

(xi) Furthermore, there is improved risk governance. The crisis has revealed weaknesses in risk governance and lack of risk experience and skills amongst executive management. Indeed, the risk management structure has seen improved support from senior management. More scrutiny on the expertise, skill and knowledge of the risk managers is a logical next step.

(xii) Approach, technology and culture of risk are also evolving. Integrated, also called Enterprise Risk Management (ERM) approach to risk management is the new trend. In this case, risk is measured across the whole institutions not based on a departmental siloed approach. The interconnectedness among all risk type is fully explored so as to capture correlations.

(xiii) The activities of insurance firms are of major concern to other financial market participants. Insurance firms are interconnected with pension funds, banks and brokers. They provide risk management services to most banks hence, their risk management practices are a major concern to other market participants. Fortunately, insurance firms have always been at the forefront of sophisticated risk analytics, especially in modelling extreme scenarios, catastrophes and dependence both within and outside the financial sector. Solvency II and its variants are used by regulators to monitor the activities of the insurance sector.

1.7   Conclusion

Risk management has been a long-standing practice in the financial service industry as well as other industries. The considerable number of risks faced by financial markets underscores the need for effective risk management in order to ensure stability of the financial system. Stability of the financial system is a major challenge to regulators given the effect insolvency of financial institutions can have on the economy and beyond.

The Nigerian financial regulators, led by the CBN are at the forefront of modern risk management. Indeed, the CBN is not only strongly imposing Basel II (and soon Basel III) regulatory frameworks on Nigerian banks, the Apex Bank is implementing an Enterprise-Wide Risk Management System to manage the risks it faces. It is also pursuing macroprudential regulation of the financial sector and is carrying out a nation-wide stress test which ties into macro-economic forecasting. The banking sector participants should continue to look deeper into emerging risk management issues at their various institutions, knowing full well that at NDIC, complementary efforts are being made to ensure that risk management issues in the financial system are addressed with the importance that they deserve. Indeed, the NDIC has always placed a great importance on the design, development and implementation of sound risk management practices. The NDIC has, in collaboration with the CBN, already adopted risk-based supervision for examining banks while assessment of deposit insurance premiums of banks by the NDIC is based on their risk exposures. NDIC also has an integrated or enterprise risk management system in place, and is overhauling its early-warning systems for detecting distress in banks.

Reference

Audu, I. (2014), "Risk Management in Financial Service Industry", Understanding Monetary Policy Series No 040, Central bank of Nigeria, https://www.cbn.gov.ng/out/2016/mpd/understanding%20monetary%20policy%20series%20no%2040.pdf

Claessens, S., & Kose, M. M. A. (2013). Financial crises explanations, types, and implications (No. 13-28). International Monetary Fund

Global Association of Risk Professionals (GARP). (2009). *Foundations of Energy Risk Management: An overview of the energy sector and its physical and financial markets.* J. Wiley & Sons

Hull, J. (2015). *Risk Management and Financial Institutions,* Website. John Wiley & Sons

NDIC Annual Report 2007-2012 available at https://www.ndic.gov.ng/annual-reports

Sanusi, S. L. (2010), "Global financial meltdown and the reforms in the Nigerian banking sector" Speech by Governor of the Central Bank of Nigeria, at a Public Lecture delivered at the Convocation Square, Abubakar Tafawa Balewa University, Bauchi, 10 December 2010

2

THE ROLE OF MICROFINANCE BANKS IN ECONOMIC DEVELOPMENT[2]

2.0   Introduction

In both the developed and developing economies, the three primary macroeconomic policy goals are, the attainments of economic growth, full employment, and price stability. All three goals are important because of their impact on the standard of living. The goal of enhancing the standard of living of the citizenry in all economies of the world through policies on inclusive development, lowering income inequalities and achieving a balance in urban-rural development, as well as the promotion of access to ownership of productive resources, is an enduring one.

Financial intermediation plays a key role in the attainment of these broad macroeconomic goals stated

---

2   Original version of this paper was delivered at the 2nd North-East Economic Summit, 2013 held at the Government House Banquet Hall, Gombe on 3rd and 4th December, 2013.

above. Traditionally, formal financial intermediation had been limited to deposit money banks (DMBs) and development finance institutions (DFIs). But following the 1974 famine in Bangladesh, Prof. Yunus, two years later in 1976, designed and implemented microcredit and microfinance schemes to enable the poor have access to credit without the burden of collaterals required by traditional banks. The Grameen Bank model as established by Prof. Yunus, was branded as a veritable mechanism to stimulate development, especially in developing economies. Since then, microcredit and microfinance have gained worldwide acceptance as policy instruments to promote inclusive growth with emphasis on poverty reduction.

In May 2003, the Nigeria Federal Government decided to transform community banks into microfinance banks (MFBs) in order to stimulate growth and development at the grass-root level. The banks were to promote small-scale business activities. Consequently, a "Microfinance Policy, Regulatory and Supervisory Framework" was issued by the CBN in 2005, creating a platform for the establishment of MFBs and establishing a framework for the CBN, as well as other supervisory agencies, such as the NDIC, to supervise the MFBs.

The World Bank (2013) categorised microfinance institutions as those institutions which "consist of agents and organisations engaged in relatively small financial transactions using specialised, character-based methodologies to serve low income households, micro enterprises, small farmers and others who lack access to the formal financial system". It is clear from the foregoing that the focus and key objective of microfinance is poverty alleviation. However, there are many terms that are used to describe microfinance in the literature such as microcredit and microfinance, which are sometimes used interchangeably. Moreover, it is important to know that there are differences among them. According to Sinha (1998) "microcredit refers to small loans, whereas microfinance is appropriate where Microfinance Institutions (MFIs) supplement the loans with other financial services (savings, insurance, etc.)". Accordingly, microcredit is an element of microfinance, whereas the main goal of microfinance is to provide credit to the core poor persons in the society. Microfinance services generally include savings and credit but can also offer payment services. In addition to financial intermediation, many microfinance institutions provide social intermediation services such as group formation, training in financial literacy and management capabilities among members of a group. Thus, the roles of microfinance banks also include both financial and social intermediation.

Today, the role of microfinance in economic development has taken a centre stage in economic planning and strategy refinement across global economies. This is because of the realisation that the credit facilities provided to small businesses/enterprises by microfinance institutions can become catalysts for their growth, employment and poverty reduction. The role of microfinance is considered to be of particular importance here because Nigeria's economy is dominated by small and medium scale enterprises in agriculture, manufacturing, commerce and industry services (Nwankwo and Ewuim, 2012), much of which operate in the informal sector, but still seen as the backbone of the economy and key sources of economic growth, dynamism and flexibility (Mahmoud, 2005).

It is in this regard that credit interventions of microfinance institutions become critical for accelerating growth in domestic output and broadening and deepening the material and social welfare of citizens. The micro-finance policy for Nigeria is aimed at expanding financial infrastructure of the country to meet the financial requirements of the poor, low-income groups and micro-entrepreneurs. Serving such groups is expedient for three reasons (CBN, 2005). First, such services create benefits to the poor through provision of increased employment opportunities, reduction in poverty and vulnerability, empowerment, improved educational and nutritional level of family members, and better access to goods and services. Secondly, the micro-entrepreneurs constitute a target group to which micro-finance institutions could provide profitable service. Thirdly, it provides better economic opportunities for both clients and financial institutions that lead to growth and development of the entire economy.

The remainder of this chapter focuses on the experiences so far in the development of microfinance in Nigeria and the regulatory role of the NDIC.

2.1 Microfinance Policy Objectives in Nigeria

The Federal Government, through the CBN, in December 2005 released Microfinance Policy, Regulatory and Supervisory Framework, which were revised in September 2013 to further enhance the provision of diversified microfinance services to the active poor and low-income earners on a sustainable basis.

The critical roles of MFBs as contained in the Microfinance Policy included the:

a) Provision of diversified, affordable and dependable financial services to the active poor, in a timely and competitive manner, that would enable beneficiaries undertake and develop long-term, sustainable entrepreneurial activities;

b) Mobilisation of savings for intermediation;

c) Creation of employment opportunities and an increase in the productivity of the active poor in the country, thereby raising their individual household income and uplifting their standard of living;

d) Enhancement of organised, systematic and focused participation of the poor in socio-economic development and resource allocation;

e) Provision of veritable avenues for the administration of the micro-credit programmes of government and high net-worth individuals on a non-recourse case basis; and

f) Rendering of payment services, such as salaries, gratuities, and pensions for various tiers of government.

In furtherance of the above, policy targets were set in the framework and they included:

a) covering the majority of the poor population who are economically active by 2020 thereby creating millions of jobs and reducing poverty;

b) increasing the share of micro credits as percentage of total credit to the economy from 0.9% in 2005 to at least 20% in 2020; and the share of micro credit as a percentage of GDP from 0.2% in 2005 to at least 5% in 2020;

c) promoting the participation of at least, two-thirds of state and local governments in microcredit financing by 2015;

d) elimination of gender disparity by improving women's access to financial services by 5% annually; and

e) increasing the number of linkages among deposit money banks, development banks, specialised finance institutions and microfinance banks by 10% annually.

The licensing requirements in the Revised Microfinance Policy Framework identified three categories of MFBs:

Category 1

Unit Microfinance Bank: Is authorised to operate in one location. The minimum paid-up capital of a Unit Microfinance Bank is ₦20 million and is prohibited from having branches and/or cash centres.

Category 2

State Microfinance Bank: Is authorised to operate in one State alone or the Federal Capital Territory (FCT). It is required to have a minimum paid-up capital of ₦100 million, and is allowed to open branches within the same State or the FCT, subject to prior written approval of the CBN for each new branch or cash centre.

Category 3

National Microfinance Bank: Is authorised to operate in more than one State, including the FCT. The minimum paid-up capital required for setting up a National Microfinance Bank is ₦2 billion and is allowed to open branches in all States of the federation, including the FCT, subject to prior written approval of the CBN for each new branch or cash centre.

2.2 The Dynamic Link between Microfinance and Rural Development

Rural development emerged as a distinct focus of policy and research in the 1960s and gained full momentum in the 1970s, as it realised that, whilst economic growth and industrialisation were important, rural development was important to a country's development (Harris, 1982). The various actors involved in rural development include farmers, rural artisans, government organisations, non-governmental organisations (NGOs) , community-based organisations (CBOs), donors, rural development professionals, researchers, private firms and businesses.

Many scholars have attempted to offer a precise definition of rural development. For example, Setty (2002), stated that rural development is a 'process that is geared towards raising the living standard of people and broadening the quality of life of persons residing in the rural areas. Fernando (2008), on the other hand defined rural development as the progress achieved in expanding the quality of life of people in the rural areas to become self-reliant within their communities. Chambers (1983), sees rural development as a strategy to enable a specific group of people, poor rural women and men, to gain for themselves and their children more of what they want and need. According to the World Bank (2013), rural development covers the strategy deployed to improve the economic and social life of a specific group of people, who more often than not are the rural poor, including small and marginal farmers, tenants and the landless. Whatever the differences in these definitions, they all converge on the need to include rural peoples in the growth and development process that enhances their material welfare, give them opportunities for choices and a sense of participation in the political and social life of the community and country.

The transformational role of microfinance in this inclusive development process, by empowering the rural dwellers with the much-needed capital to start a profitable business, whether small manufacturing, trading and provision of other services in their communities cannot be overemphasised. The schema below depicts the nexus between microfinance and inclusive rural development. The economic dimension encompasses providing both capacity and opportunities for the poor and low-income rural households to participate in and benefit from the economic growth process and measures to reduce intra- and inter-sectoral income inequalities to reasonable levels. The social dimension seeks to provide support meant to minimise inequalities in social indicators, promoting gender equality and women's empowerment, and providing social safety-nets for the vulnerable groups. The political dimension involves building capacity and opportunities to participate in political process by the poor, including women and ethnic minorities, to ensure effective representation from the village level to the larger community and national levels.

Figure 2.1: Interrelationship between Microfinance and Rural Development.

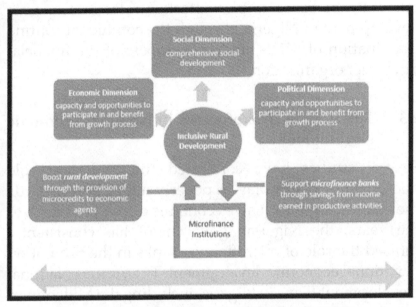

Source: NDIC, Modified from Fernando (2008)

It is well established that "empowerment" is closely related to development as it connotes an increase in economic strength of a people. Rural development and empowerment are therefore critical ingredients for alleviating poverty and ensuring a society's economic growth and transformation. To achieve all these, the provision of funds through microfinance banks is considered a critical input.

Indeed, Muhammad Yunus of the Grameen Bank in Bangladesh noted succinctly that "microfinance is a potent anti-poverty tool" without which participation, a country like Nigeria might not realise the goals of sustainable economic development. And Nigeria is in dire need of rural transformation and empowerment of the teeming rural dwellers. For this reason, the NDIC and CBN have resolved to systematically position microfinance banks to play effective roles in economic development of Nigeria, through the conduct of routine examination of MFBs, and as members of the financial safety-net organisation.

2.3 The Role of Microfinance in National Economic Development

Several studies have confirmed the important role microfinance banks play in poverty alleviation towards the attainment of inclusive economic development. Over the years, the Nigerian government has consistently infused the role of microfinance banks in the promotion of national economic development. The various National Development Plans in Nigeria, including the Millennium Development Goals (MDGs)/Sustainable Development Goals (SDGs), the National Economic Empowerment and Development Strategy (NEEDS) and the Vision 2020; were intrinsically designed with the aim of assisting the core-poor in the society to gain financial freedom through specialised programmes and initiatives that include microfinance.

MFBs are therefore strategically positioned to expand the financial frontiers and stimulate the development of economic opportunities in the informal sector. Thus, MFBs can provide traditional and even non-traditional banking services, such as technical and managerial assistance, sale of output and input purchase financing, machinery and equipment leasing and community development financing. The MFBs are therefore the cornerstone in the promotion of rural development through financial inclusion and financial literacy, deposit mobilisation and credit delivery to finance micro-enterprises, boosting small-scale enterprises and agriculture through direct financing or by acting as channels for on-lending funds to beneficiaries. They can thus create employment, promote entrepreneurship, provide skills and facilitate the various initiatives of the federal government in poverty reduction. In this regard, the CBN's ₦220 billion facility launched in 2013, for Micro, Small and Medium-Scale Enterprises Development Fund (MSMEDF) will be accessed by MFBs for onward lending to micro and medium enterprises. A number of new initiatives rolled out by the federal government, including agency banking, whose guidelines were released in February 2013 will further expand the role of the MFBs in credit giving. Under the initiative, for example, an MFB can appoint agents (a retail or postal outlet) to process customers' transactions on its behalf.

The role of microfinance banks can be summarised as follows:

a) Deposit mobilisation and promotion of savings culture provides a safe place to keep and build up savings to meet several needs when they fall due, such as payment for rentage of shops, tools, accommodation, school fees, and medical expenses. MFBs facilitate savings mobilisation and loan repayments through visits to customers' homes and offices as most workers and/or entrepreneurs of micro enterprises save them the time involved in such business transactions. The interest paid by microfinance banks on savings deposits has helped to promote a healthy banking culture amongst the hitherto marginalised (unbanked) groups.

b) Credit extension to customers is perhaps one of the most important roles of MFBs, as the loans extended are the main sources of fund used to expand existing businesses and, in some cases, to start new ones. The credit delivery system in the MFBs focuses exclusively on the poor segment of the population. The borrowers are organised into small homogenous groups and are given loans to meet their diverse development needs, without the traditional emphasis on tangible collaterals. Governments also encourage co-operatives to partner with the MFBs to raise bulk loans for on-lending to the beneficiaries.

c) Employment generation to contribute to job creation in the rural areas through the provision of skills acquisition and adult literacy programmes is also an important role of the MFBs. In some cases, the MFBs may pass on new skills and production techniques, including start-up financing, to a micro enterprise under a profit-sharing agreement.

d) Promotion of entrepreneurship stresses the fact that microfinance does not only to extend credit, but promotes entrepreneurship and boost rural financial markets by creating a business relationship between those with financial resources and those with entrepreneurial skills. The MFBs also facilitate economic development by providing ancillary capacity building to micro-enterprises in areas such as record keeping and small business management; collection of money or proceeds of banking instruments on behalf of their customers through correspondent banks; and provision of payment services such as salary, gratuity and pension for the staff of micro-enterprises at various tiers of government.

Other services provided by MFBs include loan disbursement services for the delivery of credit programme of government agencies, groups and individuals for poverty alleviation on non-recourse basis; provision of ancillary banking services to their customers such as domestic remittance of funds and safe custody; and investment of surplus microfinance funds in suitable instruments including placing funds with correspondent banks and in treasury bills, amongst others. Further roles played by MFBs include: reorientation of the rural populace on sound financial practices, partnering with other institutions to provide insurance services to clients, reproductive healthcare, girl-child education and the granting of scholarship to children of clients up to secondary and university education (Ehgiamusoe, 2011).

2.4 The Practice of Microfinance Banking in Nigeria

Ever since the CBN released the Microfinance Policy Framework, the number of MFBs established continues to rise. Although dampened in its growth during periods of economic meltdown, the prospect for microfinance banks' growth in Nigeria remains enormous. Under this section, the zonal distribution of microfinance banks and the prospect for their growth in the country are examined.

2.4.1 Distribution of MFBS by Geo-Political Zones

The number of MFBs with operational licence stood at 1,008 as at the end of 2017, representing an increase of

5.9% and 3.1% over the figures recorded in 2015 and 2016, respectively. From Table 2.1, South-West Zone, like previous years, had the highest number of operational MFBs, totalling 361 or 35.81% of the total, followed by North-Central (184) and South-East (177). The North-East Zone had the lowest number of MFBs in the country, with only 42 MFBs, which is a decline of 14.29% and 8.69% from the figures recorded in 2015 and 2016, respectively. The reason for the observed decrease in the number of MFBs in the zone could be attributed to the impact of security challenges in the region which had resulted in widespread displacement, hunger and devastation in the zone.

Table 2.1: Distribution of MFBs by Geo-Political Zones (2015 – 2017)

Geo-Political Zone	2015		2016		2017	
	No. of MFBs	%	No. of MFBs	%	No. of MFBs	%
South-West	334	35.12	341	34.86	361	35.81
South-South	108	11.36	110	11.25	112	11.11
South-East	172	18.09	173	17.69	177	17.56
North-West	123	12.93	114	11.66	132	13.1
North-East	49	5.15	46	4.7	42	4.17
North-Central	165	17.35	194	19.84	184	18.25
Total	951	100	978	100	1008	100

Source: NDIC Annual Report 2017

2.4.2 Participation of MFBs in the Disbursement of Micro, Small and Medium Enterprises Development Fund (MSMEDF)

In line with its developmental functions and mandate of promoting a sound financial system in Nigeria, the CBN launched a ₦220 billion MSMEDF on 15th August, 2013. That was in recognition of the invaluable contributions of the Micro, Small and Medium Enterprises (MSME) sub-sector to the economy. It is crucial to note that 60% of the Fund was earmarked for providing financial services to women to try to close the gender disparity.

Under the Framework, provision was made for each of the 36 states and the FCT to be entitled to access, as much as ₦2 billion from the funds, but only through Participating Financial Institutions (PFIs) in the states, which are expected to affect the disbursements directly to the beneficiaries. Also, the fund is sourced at 3% and disbursed at 9%. As at 31st December, 2016, the sum of ₦52.34 billion had been disbursed to various institutions.

2.4.3 Challenges and Prospects for Microfinance Banks Growth in Nigeria

The development of microfinance institution is constrained by such time-bound factors as weak board oversight and poor governance, weak capital base and paucity of funds, high operating costs, poor asset quality and dearth of experienced and skilled staff. Other limiting factors include weak capacity building process, poor rendition of returns and low level management information system, low literacy level and the challenge of premium administration, high number of customer complaints, among others.

In spite of these challenges, the potentials for developing the microfinance institution is enormous. Recent data from the EFInA's Access to Financial Services in Nigeria, (2016), survey showed that, 40.1 million adults, representing 41.6% of the adult population were financially excluded. Only 36.9 million adults were banked, representing 38.3% of the adult population in the year under reference. The report also showed that South-East and South-South exclusion rates of 28% and 31%, respectively are closer to the national target of 20% exclusion rate by 2020, compared to North-East and North-West with exclusion rate of 62% and 70%, respectively. The on-going security challenge in the north has added its own constraint to the expansion of microfinance banks in the region. So far, only the South-West geo-political zone has achieved the National Financial Inclusion Strategy target of reducing the proportion of adults that are financially excluded to 20% ahead of the target date of 2020.

Also, EFInA report showed that, access to finance in Nigeria is critically skewed toward the male adults, suggesting that adult men are more likely to be banked than adult women. The result thus, indicated that adult women tend to use more 'formal other' and 'informal' financial services than adult men. Additionally, the result indicates that 26 to 35 age bracket has the highest population, but ranked second in formal financial inclusion. The highest level of formally included are in the 36 to 45 age bracket, while the highest level of financially excluded are in the 18 to 25 age bracket, which aptly represents the average schooling age range in Nigeria. That distribution presents huge opportunity for deposit money banks and other financial system stakeholders to design financial products for this group of individuals to significantly reduce the proportion of the population excluded from financial services.

2.5 The Role of NDIC in Repositioning MFBs

NDIC has been fully supportive of MFBs to ensure they are profitably sustainable, so that their role in attaining the policy objectives of inclusive growth and development of our economy is realised. It is for this reason that the Corporation conducts routine examination on the MFBs to ascertain their soundness and safety, provide deposit guarantee, financial and technical assistance, support financial literacy and adopt depositor-friendly failure resolution mechanisms.

In a bid to boost confidence and operations, NDIC in January 2008 extended deposit insurance cover to microfinance banks and in 2010, reviewed upwards the deposit insurance coverage from ₦100,000 to ₦200,000.

The NDIC, in collaboration with the CBN and Chartered Institute of Bankers of Nigeria (CIBN), in 2009, commenced the Microfinance Certification Programme (MCP) for the Board, Executive and operators of MFBs to upscale capacity building in the MFB sub-sector. That was another mechanism of ensuring mandatory continuing education scheme.

2.6 Conclusion

The prospects for growth in microfinance banking activities remained potent in Nigeria owing to vast proportion of her population residing in the rural areas. Only 36.9 million adults were banked, representing 38.3% of the adult population in 2016 (EFinA, 2016).

Between 2014 and 2016, the adult population growth outpaced the growth in the banked population as the number of the financially excluded population grew from 36.9 million in 2014 to 40.1 million in 2016. EFInA 2016 Report showed that access to finance in Nigeria was critically skewed toward the male adults, leaving a huge gap for the vast number of females without access to formal financial services.

The performance of the microfinance sub-sector is impaired by inherent systemic challenges, but the potential for expanding the microfinance institution in Nigeria is enormous. For this reason, the NDIC will continue to help MFBs build public confidence in their operations in the national quest to enhance economic development.

References

Central Bank of Nigeria, CBN (2005). Microfinance Policy, Regulatory and Supervisory Framework for Nigeria, Central Bank of Nigeria Abuja, December 2005. Retrieved: http://www.cbn.gov.ng/out/publications/guidelines/dfd/2006/microfinance%20policy.pdf

Chambers, R.(1983). *Rural Development: Putting the Last First*. Harlow, Longman

Ehigiamusoe, G. (2011). *Issues in Microfinance: Enhancing Financial Inclusion*, Mindex Publishing, Benin-Nigeria

Enhancing Financial Innovation & Access, EFInA, (2016). EFInA Access to Financial Services in Nigeria 2014 Survey." Key Findings available at: http://www.efina.org.ng/assets/A2F/2016/Key-Findings-A2F-2016.pdf

Fernando, N.A., (2008). *Rural Development Outcomes and Drivers*, Asian Development Bank, pp. 4-6

Harriss, J. (1982). *Rural Development: Theories of Peasant Economy and Agrarian Change*. Hutchinson University Library for Africa, London

Kefas, S. D. (2006). Fighting Poverty through Empowering Women with Microfinance. *A Quarterly Newsletter of International Year of Microcredit*, 2(1)

Mahmoud, D. (2005). Private Sector Development and Poverty Reduction in Nigeria: Mainstreaming the Small Medium Enterprises Sector, *The Nigeria Economic Submit Group (NESG) Economic Indicators*, 11(1), 18 – 23

NDIC, (Various Years). Nigeria Deposit Insurance Corporation: Annual Reports, Abuja: NDIC

Nwankwo, F. and Ewuim, N. (2012). Role of Cooperatives in Small and Medium Scale Enterprises (SMEs) Development in Nigeria: Challenges and the Way Forward. *African Research Review*, 6 (4), 140-156

Setty, E.D., (2002). *A New Approach to Rural Development*, Anmol Publication Pvt. Ltd, pp. 1-38

Sinha, S. (1998). Microcredit: Introduction and review. *IDS Bulletin*, 29 (4), 1–9

Todaro, M. P. and Smith, S. C. (2015). *Economic Development* (12th Edition), Pearson (2015)

World Bank, (2013). *The New Microfinance Handbook: A Financial Market System Perspective*, Washington DC: World Bank

Yunus, Muhammad (2007). *Creating a World without Poverty: Social Business and the Future of Capitalism*. New York: Public Affairs. ISBN 978-1-58648-493-4

3

MOBILE PAYMENT SERVICES IN NIGERIA[3]

3.0   Introduction

The Central Bank of Nigeria (CBN) and the NDIC, as regulators have been leading the way in the Nigerian financial inclusion drive. The CBN and other stakeholders are implementing the National Financial Inclusion Strategy (NFIS) which commenced in 2012, to increase the percentage of adult Nigerians in financial services from the current 46.3% to 80% by 2020, in line with the Maya Declaration at the 2011 Alliance for Financial Inclusion (AFI) Global Policy Forum held in Mexico.

According to the 2016 report produced by Enhancing Financial Innovation and Access (EFInA), Nigeria's adult population stood at 96.4 million of which 59.7 million or 61.9% are rural. And of this rural population, about 31.2 million or 52.2% are financially excluded. With the rising trend in the ownership of mobile phones in Nigeria,

---

3   Original version of this paper was presented at the occasion of the Roundtable Discussion on Mobile Payment Services in Nigeria at Intercontinental Hotel, Victoria Island, Lagos, June 12, 2014.

mobile payment services can be a key mechanism for promoting financial inclusion in line with the objectives of NFIS, and as achieved in Kenya, Uganda and South Africa. The regulatory and supervisory authorities, in conjunction with the operators in the banking and finance industry in Nigeria, are determined and committed to reducing the number of the unbanked adult population by implementing policies that promote financial inclusion through mobile payment services.

Mobile payment basically refers to payment services operated under financial regulation and performed via a mobile device. Mobile devices are a convenient, secure and affordable way to purchase, send and receive money (NDIC, 2015). Consequently, mobile phones are attractive ways for promoting financial inclusion, given their extensive presence in the country's population. In fact, the confluence of banking technologies with mobile telephony, leads to wider penetration and holds new promise of financial inclusion for the unbanked.

It is against this backdrop that this chapter analyses mobile payment services generally and specifically in the context of Nigeria. Section 3.1 of the chapter discusses the economic purpose and technological interface of mobile payment services; Section 3.2 presents the characteristics and operational models of mobile payments system; Section 3.3 provides a brief on overall regulatory framework for mobile payment services in Africa; Section 3.4 presents the roles of the NCC, CBN and NDIC as the regulatory authorities in Nigeria; Section 3.5 presents some challenges facing the mobile payment services in Nigeria and Section 3.6 concludes the chapter.

3.1 Economic Purpose and Technological Interface of Mobile Payment

3.1.1 Economic Purpose of Mobile Payments

Flood *et al* (2013) opined that mobile payments aid two categories of economic and financial activities:

i. Purchases: These are mobile payments in exchange for goods and services. Purchases can either be through point-of-sale or remotely. The former is when the payer and the payee are in the same location, using a mobile instrument like the ATM, for example as a means of transaction, while the latter is when the payer and the payee are in different locations, employing a similar instrument like a mobile telephone.

ii. Transfers/Remittances: These are unilateral transfers from one party to the other that do not create an obligation for or extinguish an obligation to the benefitting party. This type of payment is common in developing countries as it includes both domestic and cross-border remittances based on a mobile money model.

3.1.2 Technological Interface of Mobile Payment

In the mobile payment literature, three main ways have been identified to initiate payments on a mobile device (Flood *et al*, 2013):

i. SMS or Unstructured Supplementary Service Data (USSD): This is a situation whereby a message is sent by the user through the mobile phone network to initiate a payment. This channel of mobile payment is commonly used for remote money transfer payments. USSD is a mobile messaging service unlike the SMS that exchanges messages in a real-time open session.

ii. Mobile Internet: This is a process whereby the mobile device affords platform for accessing the internet and initiating payments via the mobile device through a Web application (App) or internet banking system.

iii. Contactless or Near Field Communication (NFC): This is where a mobile device, aided with an NFC chip, is placed close to an NFC-supported terminal and payment information is transmitted via radio frequencies.

3.1.3 List of Mobile Payment Systems

Table 3.1 presents some of the mobile payment systems used in some selected countries.

Table 3.1: Mobile Payment Systems in some Selected Countries

Product	Operator	Description	Country
M-Pesa	Safaricom	It enables consumers to make personal transfers, ATM withdrawals, pay bills, make POS purchases and also allows top-up of mobile account	Kenya
Wizzit	South Africa Bank of Athens Ltd.	It offers services such as personal transfers, mobile account top-up, electricity vouchers.	South Africa

Smart Money	Smart	Allows personal transfers, bill payments, top-up, receive international remittances, linked to Mastercard for ATM, POS purchases	Philippines
Digicel Mobile Money	Digicel	Allows personal payments, top-up, receive international remittances, bill payment.	Samoa, Fiji, Tonga
MiCash	Nationwide Microbank	Allows top-up, balance inquiry, personal transfers, deposits and withdrawals.	Papua New Guinea
PayPal	eBay	Allows linking of bank accounts, credit or debit cards, use funds in a PayPal account, Instore payments, personal transfers.	Available in over 200 countries
Google Wallet	Google	Allow both online and POS purchases through debit and credit cards or NFC technology.	USA, China, Canada, UK, etc.

Source: Flood *et al* (2013)

3.2 Characteristics and Operational Models of Mobile Payment System

3.2.1 Characteristics of Mobile Payment System

Rushabh *et al* (2015) identified five features that a mobile payment services should possess:

i. Universal Usage: The payment system should facilitate ease of transactions between customers or between owners or between customers and owners. Also, the system should be globally acceptable and useable, irrespective of the location. Coverage is expected to include domestic, regional and global environments.

ii. Cost Effectiveness: The mobile payment system should be cost effective relative to existing payment system. Consequently, its operational cost should not be more than existing mechanisms.

iii. Speed: The promptness of the mobile system in terms of execution should be acceptable to both customers and merchants. It is expected to be as fast as possible in terms of usage and transactions.

iv. Platform Independent (Interoperability): The mobile payment system should be developed based on acceptable global standards and technologies. Also, it should allow interface with other payment systems regarding transactions implementation.

v. Safety and Security: One key characteristic of a mobile payment system that will ensure confidence and reliability is the security features embedded into the platform. The payment platform must ensure that customers' credit or debit card information are safe and will not be misused. Also, customers' information should not be openly available to the public, therefore, the platform should be protected from hackers.

3.2.2 Mobile Payment Service Provider Models

In the literature, four potential mobile payment service provider models are identified (Chaix and Torre, 2011). These are:

i.   Operator-Centric Model is a where the telecommunication operator acts independently to set up the mobile payment service which provides the platform for the transactions to take place. The platform allows the link between payment system and bank account. The system also allows a third party to provide the liquidity and be compensated by the operator. An example is the M-Pesa model provided by Vodafone for Safaricom in Kenya.

ii. Bank-Centric Model is when a bank provides mobile payment devices to customers and guarantees that merchants have the acceptable point-of-sale (POS) technology. In the bank-centric approach, communication companies only act as the carrier link to guarantee quality of service on the payment platform. Chaix and Torre (2011) stated that the bank-centric model can be considered as an evolution of the credit card model.

iii. Collaboration Model allows a collaboration among communication operators, banks and the participation of a trusted third party. The third party provides the link between the bank and the operators and every partner derives their benefits from fees charged to both merchants and final users. A good example is the secured mobile payment system (SEMOPS) model in Europe which acts as a third party in managing the link between banks and communication operators. The users of the service only sign deals with their bank or their mobile phone providers to use the service, as there is no need to have any direct deal with SEMOPS.

iv. Independent Service Provider Model is when a third party that is neither a financial agent nor communication/phone operator provides an intermediary role between banks, phone operators, traders and final users in guaranteeing payment transactions. An example is PayPal by eBay or GPay by Google.

3.3 Regulatory Framework for Mobile Payment Services

The African policymakers and regulators, as members of the AFI, met in Zanzibar, Tanzania on 15 February, 2013 to launch and hold the inaugural Leaders Roundtable Meeting of the first African Mobile Phone Financial Services Policy Initiative (AMPI). The purpose of AMPI was to establish or extend existing Mobile Financial Services (MFS) policy and regulatory frameworks to expand the penetration of MFS Africa-wide. That was to be done in line with national policy priorities through cooperation among policy makers, regulators, private sector players, development partners as well as research institutions. The AMPI represents the first African regional effort to tackle the challenge of bringing the continent's unbanked population into the formal financial system. The AMPI comprises central banks from the African region as members. The NDIC is an associate member, whose membership was supported by the CBN. Both CBN and NDIC actively participated in the 2nd Leaders Roundtable of AMPI held in Kenya in February 2014.

3.4 Highlights of the Responsibilities of the Regulators in Nigeria

In Nigeria, the NCC, CBN and the NDIC are the main regulators for mobile payment services. The NCC covers communication/phone service providers, CBN is in charge of financial service providers, and NDIC is responsible for the pass-through deposit insurance for subscribers of MMOs. The highlights of each regulator is provided below:

3.4.1 *The Nigerian Communication Commission and Mobile Payment Services*

The Nigerian Communications Commission (NCC) as an independent national regulatory authority for the telecommunications industry, is responsible for the regulation and supervision of all infrastructure required to support mobile payment services in Nigeria. In conjunction with the CBN, NCC specifies the minimum technical and business requirements for the various participants in the industry.

To achieve the financial inclusion objective, the CBN signed an MOU with the NCC to allow digital mobile operators incorporate Special Purpose Vehicles (SPVs) to offer mobile money services to customers. A joint technical committee was then raised by the NCC and the CBN to work out the modalities for the implementation of the MoU so that the mobile communication operators through the use of the SPVs would become formal mobile money operators.

The CBN had already issued the Super Agents Licensing Framework to encourage other infrastructure providers and operators to provide shared agent network services. Consequently, the CBN had granted an approval-in-principle to Innovectives Limited and Interswitch Financial Inclusion Services Limited to operate as super agents in the financial services system.

3.4.2 The Central Bank of Nigeria and Mobile Payment Services

The CBN is responsible for defining and monitoring the Mobile Payment Systems in Nigeria. Pursuant to its mandate of promoting a sound payment system, it issued guidelines for mobile payment services to promote and facilitate the development of efficient and effective system for the settlement of transactions, including the development of electronic payment systems. The CBN in collaboration with other relevant stakeholders drafted and released the regulatory framework for mobile payment services in Nigeria in 2009. Some of the specific responsibilities of the CBN include the use of operational models and MMO capitalisation.

3.4.2.1 Operational Models: Bank and Non-bank Models

There are two operational models for mobile payment services recognised by the CBN framework:

i. *Bank-led Model*: This is a model where a bank either alone or a consortium of banks, whether partnering with other approved organisations, seek to deliver banking services, leveraging on the mobile payments system.

ii. *Non-Bank-led Model*: This model allows a corporate organisation that has been duly licensed by the CBN, to deliver Mobile Money Services to customers. The lead initiator shall be a corporate organisation (other than a deposit money bank or a telecommunication company), specifically licensed by the CBN to provide mobile money services in Nigeria.

3.4.2.2 MMO Capitalisation

According to the CBN (2009) regulatory framework, MMOs shall:

i. Be licensed by the CBN on such terms and conditions as may be prescribed from time to time.

ii. Be issued a unique Scheme Code by the NIBSS for managing interoperability.

iii. Be issued short codes by the NCC.

iv. Ensure that all telecommunication equipment are type approved by the NCC.

v. Register users of its scheme based on technology standards and the requirements of these Guidelines.

vi. Ensure that the registration processes within its mobile payments scheme shall fulfil the entire KYC requirements specified in these Guidelines.

vii. The types of card-driven payments recognised by the framework are: credit, debit and prepaid.

The initial capital base per MMO of ₦500 million was raised to ₦2 billion with effect from 1st June, 2016. This implies that each MMO should obtain a minimum shareholders' fund of ₦2 billion, unimpaired by any losses. Any MMO that could not comply with the minimum capital requirement has the option to merge with other MMOs, or else, have its licence suspended or revoked (EFinA, 2016).

3.4.3. The Nigeria Deposit Insurance Corporation and Mobile Payment Services

The NDIC provides a unique role of enhancing financial inclusion by encouraging mobile financial services because of the assurance given to low-income earners that their deposits are safe and available at all times. The deposit insurance provided to small depositors/savers, attracts the otherwise unbanked population and thus promotes financial inclusion and formal banking services. One of NDIC's critical yardsticks of success is, therefore, the extent of satisfaction of a large number of small depositors.

3.4.3.1 Promotion of financial literacy

The NDIC is equally actively involved in promoting financial literacy and supporting agent banking and non-interest/Islamic banking, as strategies for attaining financial inclusion in the country to improve the economic well-being of people who have been excluded from the formal financial system. Furthermore, Nigeria, being a predominantly cash-based society caused the NDIC to support the Cashless Policy of the CBN because of the need to modernise Nigeria's payment system, reduce the cost of banking services, drive financial inclusion, improve effectiveness of monetary policy, reduce the high security and safety risks, reduce high subsidy, foster transparency, curb corruption and ultimately meet the Federal Government's financial inclusion rate of 80% by 2020.

3.4.3.2 Pass-Through Deposit Insurance

The Pass-Through Deposit Insurance (PTDI) was introduced in Nigeria by the Corporation in June 2015 to provide deposit insurance coverage to subscribers of MMOs in order to engender confidence in the use of mobile payment platform and promote financial inclusion. Accordingly, there are 4 main thrusts of the system. These are to:

i.   guarantee the payment of insured sums to subscribers of MMOs in the event of failure of insured institutions where MMOs maintain Pool accounts;

ii. enhance confidence and ensure continuous sustenance of the MPS;

iii. protect and ensure safety and stability of the MPS; and

iv. promote financial inclusion.

Prior to the release of the guidelines, the subscribers of an MMO were not entitled to their insured amount if a bank failed. The pool account was regarded as one account, not identifying the individual subscribers and as such, was only insured up to the maximum amount of ₦500,000 per account. That left a lot of subscribers worried about their funds with MMOs. The introduction of the concept of pass-through deposit insurance makes it possible to insure an individual subscriber up to a maximum of ₦500,000 so long as such subscriber makes up the pool account.

In order to be eligible, the following criteria must be met.

i.   A Bare Trust agreement between the MMO and subscribers – which is an agreement where the beneficiary has absolute right to their funds within the pool account.

ii. MMOs must take out fidelity bond insurance to protect against losses due to insider fraud.

iii. The records of the pool account holder at the insured institution must clearly state that the account holder is a custodian and that the funds belong to individual subscribers.

iv. The identities of the subscribers are disclosed in records maintained by the insured institutions, MMOS and Agents.

v.   And all KYC requirements on the subscribers are fully met.

Since the roll-out of the framework in June 2015, the NDIC has met with MMOs and their subscribers to enlighten them on the implementation and its potential benefits. The Corporation has also gone on public awareness campaigns at trade-fairs, financial inclusion sensitisation programmes with other regulators and other mass media channels, educating the public (rural and urban) about the development of PTDI. The hope is that mass awareness will engender confidence and widen the use of mobile money services in the country.

The NDIC also developed a recording template which has been shared with MMOs to enable them render monthly and quarterly data to the Corporation for supervisory purposes. The MMOs have commenced the rendition of returns to the NDIC via the template.

3.5 Challenges Facing the Mobile Payment Services in Nigeria

The CBN issued the regulatory framework for the operations of Mobile Payments Services in Nigeria in June 2009 as a strategy to reduce the number of unbanked Nigerians in fostering financial inclusion. This Mobile Payment initiative, however, presents new challenges, part of which is the safety and security of the depositor's fund in the digital and new virtual environment. The achievements recorded since 2011, when CBN first issued 11 provisional licenses for mobile payments services to commence in Nigeria was attributable to increase in the number of mobile money operators and improved public awareness in the use of mobile banking services.

Despite the huge potential of mobile money for enhanced financial inclusion in Nigeria, its impact had been largely negligible. Since its introduction in 2011, only 1% of adults use mobile money as of 2016 (EFInA, 2017). Compared to Kenya and other emerging markets, its adoption to resolve financial exclusion had been challenging despite increasing efforts of regulators like the CBN, NDIC and NCC.

According to the 2016 EFInA report, the main reason for the low adoption of mobile money in Nigeria is the lack of knowledge and trust in mobile money services by the public. Other factors are the rather stringent regulations, lack of interoperability, inadequate infrastructure. As of June 2017, there were 21 licensed MMOs in Nigeria, 2.3 million MMO customers and 5,517 MMO agents enrolled (NIBSS E-Payments, 2017).

Despite the relatively low adoption of MMO services, transactions on the platform have been on a steady increase. For instance, Table 3.2 showed the e-payment channels volume and value of transactions at end-December, 2012 to end-June 2017. It is evident from the table that total value of transaction which stood at ₦2,070.71 billion increased to ₦3,405.14 billion in December 2013. It maintained the same trend and increased to ₦7,084.19 billion in June 2017. Despite the increase in the value of total e-payment services for the period in Nigeria, the value of transaction via mobile payment is still relatively small when compared with the increased use of mobile phones in the country.

Payment Systems	2012 December	2013 December	2014 December	2015 December	2016 December	2017 June
ATM Transactions	37,103,463	28,831,101	39,284,012	43,687,863	61,958,258	60,307,952.00
ATM Transactions (₦'Billion)	205.05	296.30	387.37	402.35	572.94	509.89
POS Transactions	478,137	1,466,154	2,636,865	3,946,721	8,994,764	11,220,631.00
POS Transactions (₦'Billion)	9.43	24.83	39.42	53.45	107.62	107.66
Web Transactions	203,651	403,830	590,922	912,521	1,798,275	1,788,583.00
Web Transactions (₦'Billion)	2.92	5.03	8.44	11.94	14.75	11.31
Mobile Payment Transactions	500,980	1,314,479	2,146,670	4,517,553	4,824,604	3,985,563.00
Mobile Payment Transactions (₦'Billion)	8.09	23.75	49.54	58.8185.85	84.37	

NIBSS Instant Payment Transactions	772,690	2,497,080	5,076,147	8,330,211	22,740,509	28,458,092.00
NIBSS Instant Payment Transactions (₦'Billion)	588.78	1,419.88	2,117.01	2,394.89	4,345.83	4,339.31
NIBSS Electronic Fund Transfer Transactions	2,772,443	3,184,013	3,049,143	2,726,740	3,183,318	3,417,291.00
NIBSS Electronic Fund Transfer Transactions (₦'Billion)	1,256.44	1,635.35	1,291.86	1,135.03	1,286.59	2,031.65
Total Volume	41,831,364	37,696,657	52,783,759	64,121,609	103,499,728	109,178,112
Total Value (₦'Billion)	2,070.71	3,405.14	3,893.64	4,056.47	6,413.58	7,084.19

Source: CBN Statistical Database

For instance, mobile payment transactions as shown in Table 3.2 and Figure 3.2 indicated that the value of transaction stood at ₦8.09 billion as at December, 2012 representing about 0.4% share of the total value of e-payment transactions. That increased slightly to ₦23.75 billion but represented a slight increase to 0.7% share in the total e-payment value of transaction as at December, 2013. In December, 2014 the value of mobile payment transaction increased to ₦49.54 billion which accounted for about 1.3% of the total value of e-payment transactions in the same period. The same trend persisted and as at June 2017, the value of mobile payment transactions increased to ₦84.37 billion representing a slight decline of its share in the previous year to 1.2% of the total value of e-payment transactions.

Figure 3:1

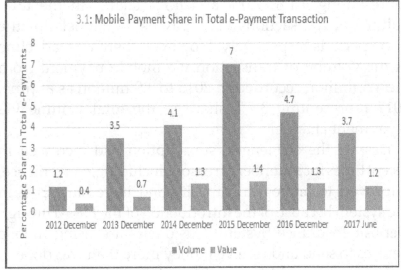

Similarly, the volume of e-payment transactions had been on the increase from 2012 to 2017 except in 2013. The total volume of e-payment transactions as shown in

Table 3.2 recorded 41.8 million volumes as at December, 2012 which fell slightly to 37.7 million transactions at end-December, 2013. The total volume of transactions however trended upward to 52.8 million as at December 2014 and maintained this upward trend to 109.2 million transactional volumes at end-June 2017. From Table 3.2 and Figure 3.1, the volume of transaction via mobile payment showed an increasing trend but had a minimal share in the total e-payment volume of transactions. For instance, as at December 2012, mobile payment recorded about 500,980 volume of transaction which represented about 1.2% share of the total. Mobile payment volume of transaction increased to 1.3 million or 3.5% of the total as at December, 2013.

Mobile payment transaction volume maintained this upward trend to 2.1 million, 4.5 million and 4.8 million as at December 2014, 2015 and 2016, respectively representing 4.1%, 7.0% and 4.7% shares in the total volume of transactions via e-payment channels for the same periods respectively. However, there was a decline in the volume of transaction via mobile payment from the 4.5 million recorded in 2016 to 3.9 million as at June, 2017 representing 3.7% share in the total volume via e-payment channels.

Despite the challenges, subscription had increased in recent times for a number of reasons including, convenience, improved technological capacity and increasing trust in the system because of the introduction of the Pass-Through Deposit Insurance System. Customers are using mobile devices to send and receive money more than was done in the past. This had improved transfers and remittances to people in rural locations.

3.6 Conclusion

The regulatory and supervisory authorities in conjunction with the operators in banking and finance industry in Nigeria are making conscious efforts at enhancing financial inclusion by implementing pro-active policies to encourage mobile payment services in Nigeria. Several initiatives have been implemented by the CBN and the NDIC to support the growth of mobile payment services in Nigeria. The CBN released the regulatory framework and licensed MMOs, while NDIC has provided insurance coverage for subscribers of mobile money.

Despite the moderate penetration of mobile money in Nigeria, there are several challenges including; the cash culture of the Nigerian public, lack of awareness of its availability and advantages, lack of trust in the platform, as well as technical and interoperability challenges hindering operators.

References

CBN (2009). CBN Regulatory Framework for Mobile Payment Services in Nigeria. https://www.cbn.gov.ng/.../exposure%20draft%20guidelines%20on%20mobile%20pa

Chaix, L. and D. Torre (2011). Four Models of Mobile Payments. http://hp.gredeg.cnrs.fr/Dominique_Torre/workpap/chaix_torre_gdr2011_17mars.pdf. Accessed on 4th April, 2018

EFInA (2016). Merger and Acquisition: Opportunities and Challenges of MMOs in the Recapilisation Era. A Paper Presented at the Mobile Money Working Group Meeting held 14th April, 2016

Enhancing Financial Innovation & Access, EFInA, (2017). Key Findings: EFInA Financial Services Agent Survey 2017. https://www.efina.org.ng/wp-content/uploads/2019/01/EFInA-Financial-Services-Agent-Survey-2017-Report.pdf

Flood, D., T. West and D. Wheadon (2013). Trends in Mobile Payments in Developing and Advanced Economies. *Bulletin,* March Quarter, 71-79

NIBSS, (2017). NIBSS E-Payment facts sheets. Jan- February 2017. www.nibss-plc.ng/epayment-fact-sheet

Rushabh, P., A. Kunche, N. Mishra, Z. Bhaiya and R. Joshi (2015). Comparative Review of Existing Mobile Payment Systems. *International Journal of Applied Engineering Research,* 10 (7): 16873-84

4

THE ROLE OF DEPOSIT INSURANCE IN PROMOTING FINANCIAL INCLUSION[4]

4.0   Introduction

As a supervisory agency that implements the Deposit Insurance Scheme in Nigeria, the NDIC plays a key role in promoting financial inclusion in the country. As a component of the Financial Safety-Net framework, deposit insurance engenders confidence in the banking industry by ensuring that banks operate in a safe and sound manner. Deposit insurance also assures depositors of their funds in the event of a bank failure. The assurance that the banks are safe and kept sound, in turn, promotes banking habit and thus, financial inclusion.

Innovative instruments such as branchless or agent banking and mobile money are employed by MFIs to expanding access to financial services and promote financial inclusion where the traditional banking model

---

4   Original version of this paper was delivered at the 1st International Conference and Doctoral Colloquium 2015 hosted by Bayero University, Kano.

has failed. With these new technological advances, the need for enhanced supervisory capacity has arisen to prevent abuse and exploitation of those taking advantage of the new banking opportunities, whose profiles often include the uneducated and the rural poor.

Section 4.1 discusses financial inclusion and poverty alleviation; while Section 4.2 discusses financial inclusion and deposit insurance; Section 4.3 presents the role of the NDIC in Nigeria's financial inclusion drive; Section 4.4 discusses the regulatory imperatives to financial inclusion and 4.5 concludes the chapter.

4.1 Financial Inclusion and Poverty Alleviation

The Bank of Tanzania defines financial inclusion as, "The regular use of financial services, through payment infrastructures to manage cash flows and mitigate shocks, which are delivered by formal providers through a range of appropriate services with dignity and fairness" (Alliance for Financial Inclusion, 2017). Generally, any definition of financial inclusion should always consider the following elements, types of financial services, providers of these services, the target group and ease of use of the services. In Nigeria, the CBN considers financial inclusion as "achieved when adult Nigerians have easy access to a broad range of formal financial services that meet their needs at affordable cost". It is generally accepted that financial inclusion has the potential to improve the livelihood of the underprivileged people across the globe. The key question to policy makers is how this can be achieved.

When households have access to credit, at affordable costs and have easy access to financial services transactions and financial channels, it stands to reason that their ability to save and thus withstand shocks improves. Consequently, the ability to save also enhances their propensity to consume, which increases economic activity in rural areas. The different financial access channels also improve the ability to transform lives. For example, the introduction of mobile money in Kenya considerably improved the earning potential of farmers. According to the World Bank Global Findex 2017, digital financial services in Kenya helped reduce extreme poverty among women-headed households by 22%.

Digital financial services, by switching from cash to digital payments, can also enhance the efficiency in the delivery of government services as they reduce avenues for corruption. In Niger, social transfers through mobile phones reduced cost of administration by 20 per cent and in India, pension payment leakages dropped by 47 per cent using a biometric smart card in place of cash payments. Mobile money and branchless banking have thus proved to be the most effective tools for financial inclusion due to the variety of financial technology available in the operation. According to World Bank 2017 Findex, the use of digital payments is trending upwards globally with the share of adults making or receiving digital payments increasing by 11 percentage points between 2014 and the percentage of people with accounts making use of digital services either in making or receiving payments has surpassed those still utilising cash in both high-income and developing economies.

4.2 Financial Inclusion and Deposit Insurance

Deposit insurance does not directly increase the level of financial inclusion, but the confidence it provides increases the likelihood of an unbanked individual opening an account with a formal service provider. Because one of the primary responsibilities of a deposit insurer is to ensure financial system stability, it must always weigh the risks associated with each financial innovation and its potential impact on financial inclusion before adoption. As such, in addition to conventional deposit money banks, microfinance banks and subscribers of mobile money are also afforded deposit protection by the NDIC, only when their new instruments are carefully analysed. In spite of these careful considerations, the following chart highlights that the contribution of the 'formal other' segment (Microfinance institutions) declined due to lack of trust in the segment accentuated by harsh economic realities. Through the various initiatives on enhancing financial inclusion, the Chart shows that the number of financially excluded persons has dropped from 45.4 million or 52.5% in 2008 to 36.9 million or 41.6% in 2016. In the same vein, the number of banked has increased from 18.3 million in 2008 to 36.9 million by 2016.

Table 4.1: **Financial Inclusion Chart**

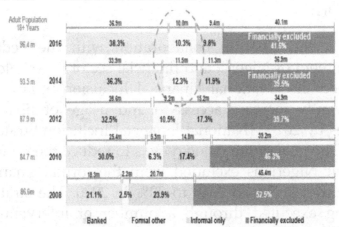

Source: EFInA Access to Financial Services in Nigeria 2008-2016 Survey

Apart from the provision of deposit coverage on financial innovations, the deposit insurer can also assist in the financial inclusion drive through:

- Public awareness campaigns, especially to reach rural areas;
- Financial literacy programmes, as rural households are often uneducated and need to be enlightened on the risks involved in financial services;
- Sound consumer protection framework to enable a reliable and fast recourse mechanism for aggrieved depositors; and
- Efficient resolution procedures to prevent disruptions in the banking system and loss of confidence.

4.3 The Role of NDIC in Nigeria's Financial Inclusion Drive

In 2012, the CBN in collaboration with the Federal Government of Nigeria and financial sector stakeholders launched the "National Financial Inclusion Strategy to significantly increase access to and usage of financial services by 2020" (National Financial Inclusion Strategy, 2012). The goal of the strategy was to reduce the number of adult Nigerians excluded from the formal financial sector from 46.3% in 2010 to 20% in 2020. The strategy is being executed through a number of interventions including, Tiered Know-Your-Customer regulations, Agent Banking and Mobile Payment Systems, Improved Credit Schemes, a National Financial Literacy Framework and a Comprehensive Consumer Protection Framework. All these interventions are expected to bring rural small savers into the formal financial system. The roles and responsibilities of the NDIC as presented elsewhere in this book and especially, as a 'Risk Minimiser', will contribute to the financial system stability and engender confidence to expand services to rural households.

Figure 4.1: **Growth in Number of Accounts of DMBs in Nigeria**

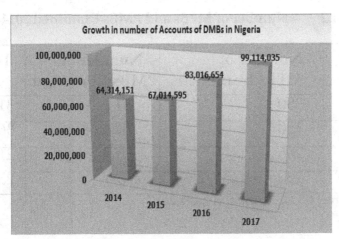

Source: NDIC Annual Report 2017

The diagram above shows, among other factors, the positive influence that deposit insurance has on confidence in the banking sector. Against the background of the NDIC's bank supervision and ensuing financial stability, the number of bank accounts have increased steadily from 64 million to 99 million between 2014 and 2017.

The NDIC has aided the National Financial Inclusion strategy of 2012 by the following activities:

i. Bank Supervision: The NDIC supervises the insured institutions through on-site examination and off-site surveillance of banks. The NDIC, in collaboration with the CBN ensures that prudential and regulatory guidelines are followed, and that customers' funds are managed safely. The Corporation conducts risk-based examination of all DMBs, PMBs and MFBs, to identify and correct weaknesses in their operations. The Table below provides details of banks examined between 2014 and 2017.

Table 4.2:   Number of MFBs and PMBs Examined 2014-2017

Year	Number of MFBs Examined	Number of PMBs Examined	Total
2017	300	10	310
2016	350	10	360
2015	205	6	211
2014	250	3	253

Source: NDIC Annual Report 2017

In addition to bank supervision, the Corporation also supervises and monitors the activities of Mobile Money Operators. Although the usage of mobile money is yet to be widely adopted, the steady growth in recent times calls for added vigilance. The graph below indicates that the value of transactions has trended upwards on digital platforms.

Figure 4.2: **Value of Transactions (₦)**

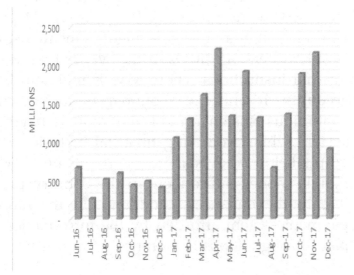

Source: NDIC Insurance & Surveillance Department

ii. **Consumer Protection:** As part of its role in promoting public confidence, the NDIC investigates complaints and petitions and has established a 24-hour Help-Desk to give depositors and other stakeholders an avenue to register their grievances. From inception, NDIC has been investigating and resolving complaints and petitions received from bank customers. The NDIC investigated 32, 47, 38 and 30 petitions/complaints received from bank customers and other stakeholders in 2014, 2015, 2016, and 2017, respectively. The complaints and allegations included ATM frauds, conversion of cheques and suppression of deposits. Like in previous years, NDIC ensured that the affected customers were appropriately reprieved, where necessary.

iii. Pass-Through Deposit Insurance: In 2015, the NDIC launched the framework for Pass-Through Deposit Insurance. It guarantees payment of insured sums to subscribers of MMOs in the event of failure of insured institutions where MMOs maintain Pool accounts. It enhances confidence and ensures continuous sustenance of the mobile payment system while promoting financial inclusion. The graph below shows increase in the number of mobile money subscribers in the country partly due to the enhanced confidence in the mobile payment system afforded by the introduction of pass-through deposit insurance.

Figure 4.3:   Number of MMO Subscribers

Source: NDIC Insurance and Surveillance Department

iv. Public Awareness: NDIC has over the years undertaken various public awareness initiatives that enhance knowledge and understanding of deposit insurance and banking in Nigeria. The public awareness activities are geared towards educating small savers of the benefits of formal financial services, the risks involved as well as the recourse mechanisms afforded to individuals who have been aggrieved by financial institutions. Some of the public awareness activities include:

a. Annual participation in major international trade fairs hosted across the country;

b. Seminars/workshops organised for staff of microfinance banks;

c. Road shows hosted for micro, small and medium scale entrepreneurs, including market men and women;

d. Radio and television programmes hosted in local languages; and

e. Publications such as journals, books on deposit insurance and banking and the easy-to-read, "Basic Knowledge on Banking and Deposit Insurance".

v. Promotion of Financial Literacy: Apart from being a member of the National Financial Inclusion Steering and Technical Committees, the NDIC has participated in key financial literacy and inclusion programmes as follows:

1. A stand-alone curriculum for financial education of Nigerian schools had been developed and implemented in partnership with CBN and the NERDC for secondary and primary schools. Furthermore, the NDIC has developed curriculum for DIS in universities in Nigeria.

2. The NDIC participated in a financial literacy training-of-trainers workshop organised by the CBN, as part of efforts to prepare for the NYSC Peer Educator Programme. The objective was for the Peer Educators to train NYSC members on Financial Inclusion/Literacy while the Corps members are to voluntarily extend the knowledge to people at the grass roots during their Community Development (CD) days. The programme was a success, as a total of 992 NYSC members were trained in 12 pilot States in November 2014. The programme was repeated in 2015 because of the success recorded in the previous year.

3. The NDIC, CBN and DMBs celebrated the 2017 World Savings Day by visiting schools in all the 36 states of the federation and the Federal Capital Territory (FCT), Abuja. Over 62,000 students were impacted by the banks with 2,678 student accounts opened during the celebrations.

4. The annual Global Money Week themed 'Learn, Earn, Save' took place from 27th March to 2nd April, 2017. Several institutions, including the NDIC, sent delegations to schools across the country to commemorate the Week.

vi. Effective Resolution Procedures: The seamless and effective resolution of failing financial institutions helps maintain and even build confidence in the sector. When the NDIC utilised the bridge-bank as a failure resolution strategy to address the problems of three failing banks, bank customers in Nigeria were unaware of the fact that their accounts had been transferred from one institution to another. That allowed normal banking operation to continue uninterrupted.

4.4   Regulatory Imperatives to Financial Inclusion

Financial inclusion cannot be achieved without appropriate financial regulation and supervisory interventions. To promote financial inclusion, regulators need to consider the risks involved with innovations and take necessary steps to mitigate the risks without hindering progress. Striking that balance becomes a major challenge for deposit insurers and central banks. In general, regulators need to pay attention to the following areas of concern:

    i. strengthen consumer protection to ensure all stakeholders feel like they have an equal voice in the industry;

    ii. address the marginalisation of women in rural societies as evidence has shown that, women are more likely to pay back loans and even save more for the household;

    iii. establish necessary infrastructure and create enabling policies for financial innovations, especially in the digital payment space;

    iv. increase monitoring activities, especially as regards developmental funds to ensure banks do not engage in round-tripping but rather transmit these funds to MSMEs; and

    v. enhance financial literacy programmes to boost financial knowledge amongst the poor and unbanked.

4.5 Conclusion

Whether or not deposit insurance can directly influence financial inclusion is a question that will require extensive study. What can be agreed upon is that, the role of deposit insurer goes beyond pay-out to include financial inclusion. Through the core principles of deposit insurance, policies and activities of deposit insurers can influence the trajectory of financial inclusion in a jurisdiction. Small savers should find confidence in deposit protection which should increase their savings culture through formal financial services providers. That in-turn will improve their opportunities for credit facilities which will increase their earning potential and ultimately help bring them out of poverty.

Several factors influence the adoption of banking by the unbanked population including, education, unemployment and availability of channels. Therefore, regulators need to consider these factors when devising a strategy to address financial exclusion in different jurisdictions. The involvement of the private sector is very critical in extending financial services to the unbanked. In developing nations, while innovative solutions are needed to reach rural households, it is also important to change their perception of formal financial services. Significant efforts need to be made to remove certain cultural stigmas of women and banks, as well as the overwhelming aura of banks being only for the wealthy. The more people are included in the formal financial sector, the greater the chance of reducing poverty and income inequality.

References

Alliance for Finance Inclusion (2017). Defining Financial Inclusion. Guidance Note No. 28

Enhancing Financial Innovation and Access (2016). Access to Financial Services Survey 2016

International Association of Deposit Insurers (2013). Financial Inclusion and Deposit Insurance. Research Paper June 2013

Nigeria Deposit Insurance Corporation Annual Report 2017

Nigeria Deposit Insurance Corporation Insurance and Surveillance Department MMO Returns

Nigeria Deposit Insurance Corporation (2015). Framework for the Establishment of Pass-Through Deposit Insurance for Subscribers of Mobile Money Operators in Nigeria

World Bank Group. The Global Findex Database 2017

5

DEPOSIT INSURANCE AND CONSUMER PROTECTION[5]

5.0   Introduction

There is now a general consensus among policy makers that stronger consumer protection, together with better financial education, is an essential pillar of a well-functioning financial system. Financial literacy is considered by policy makers as "life-skill for the 21st century" and as a "complement to financial inclusion and consumer protection policies" and as such contributes to financial stability (Muller *et al*, 2014). However, financial education, while important, is insufficient in itself to protect and empower consumers (Muller *et al*, 2014). Consumer protection is not about protecting consumers from bad decisions, but more of enabling consumers to make informed decisions in a marketplace, free of

---

5   Original version of this paper was delivered at the World Consumer Rights Day held on 15th March, 2010.

deception and abuse, which will build public confidence (FSB, 2011).

The DIS being administered by the NDIC is a financial mechanism put in place to protect depositors in the event of bank failure and also to offer a measure of safety for the banking system, thereby contributing to financial system stability. The role of the DIS, therefore, is not just in promoting confidence with explicit coverage of deposits, but also has reinforcing features that complement the supervisory process in promoting sound risk management practices in the financial institutions. This chapter aims to discuss how deposit insurance protects the consumer generally, drawing on the Nigerian experience in particular. The rest of the chapter is divided into six sections. Section 5.1 discusses the concept of and rational for deposit insurance; Section 5.2 examines the concept of consumer protection and the related regulatory framework; while Section 5.3 reflects on the efforts of the NDIC at consumer protection in Nigeria; Section 5.4 presents the challenges faced by the NDIC in consumer protection; and Section 5.5 concludes the chapter.

5.1   Concept and Rationale for Deposit Insurance

A DIS refers to the set of specific functions – whether performed by a dedicated legal entity or not – aimed at protecting banks customers against the loss of their insured deposits and networked with other financial system safety-net participants, to support financial stability (FSB, 2012). A central function of the DIS is to especially protect small depositors from the risk of loss of their deposits. Two important reasons, therefore, provide the rationale for the DIS (Pennacchi, 2009; Kleftouri, 2014):

a) it prevents bank runs, limit governments' blanket guarantees, and complement banks' resolution regimes, promotes financial stability in the economy and boosts public confidence in the banking system.

b) protects the deposits of small unsophisticated customers, who might not be aware that their deposits can be used in financing other activities, each of which has a risk attached (LaBrosse and Mayes, 2008), but for which the depositors lack the relevant information on the risk appetite of the financial institutions; or even if they did, would not likely have the expertise and resources to assess banks' appetite for risks and to take steps to protect themselves from such risks.

Depositor protection through a DIS is usually done either through explicit or an implicit arrangement. Explicit DIS entails formal deposit protection arrangement, where the terms and conditions of the scheme are explicitly stated in a statute; whereas, implicit protection involves ad-hoc arrangements instituted to reimburse depositors in times of loss due to bank failure, but without any defined parameters or backing legislature.

5.2 Concept of Consumer Protection and the Regulatory Framework

Consumer protection, in financial services, encompasses the laws, regulations, and institutional arrangements that safeguard consumers in the financial marketplace. The 2008 joint report of the Forum of the Basel Committee on Banking Supervision, the International Organization of Securities Commission and the International Association of Insurance Supervisors identified report, three key risks related to possible "mis-selling" of financial products to retail customers as legal risk, short-term liquidity, long-term solvency risk, and contagion risk.

One form of consumer protection is ensuring that financial products are made available and at the 'right' prices to all sections of the population. Another is to ensure the suitability of the products for each category of the consumer market (Lumpkin, 2010). Regulators in the field of consumer protection promote competition policy to ensure that the supply side of the economy is functioning optimally and that there is free flow of information on the demand side for informed choices by the consumer (UNCTAD, 2016). The regulator is thus faced with the responsibility of balancing the interests of consumers with those of the sellers or service providers. In this regard, the regulators can either employ the interventionist or non-interventionist approaches, or a combination of the two, to reflect possible different market structures. The interventionist approach involves monitoring the service providers which includes enforcement of business and product regulations; while non-interventionist approach allows consumers and service providers to make bargains and contracts freely without any interference from external agencies/ regulators.

It is believed amongst financial/policy analysts that there are two broad classes of regulation that affect banks: safety and soundness regulation and consumer protection regulation. While safety and soundness regulation ensures that banks and other depository institutions operate in a safe and sound manner and do not pose an excessive threat to the deposit insurance fund or taxpayers, consumer protection regulations are designed to protect the interests of consumers in their credit and other transactions with banks and financial service providers. Therefore, financial education/literacy which refers to knowledge and skills acquired by an individual to manage his/her financial resources and consumer protection policies, should form the foundation of any regulatory and supervisory framework for protecting consumers particularly, amid efforts to expand financial inclusion (FSB, 2011).

Moreover, in a bid to have common rules guiding consumer protection in the field of financial services, high-level principles on financial consumer protection were developed by the Task Force on Financial Consumer Protection of the Organisation for Economic Co-operation and Development (OECD) Committee on Financial Markets (CMF), in close co-operation with the FSB and its Consultative Group, other international organisations and standard setting bodies and consumer and industry associations. These principles were endorsed by the G20 Finance Ministers and Central Bank Governors at their meeting on 14-15 October 2011 in Paris. The ten principles are:

a) Legal, Regulatory and Supervisory Framework;
b) Role of Oversight Bodies;
c) Equitable and Fair Treatment of Consumers;
d) Disclosure and Transparency;
e) Financial Education and Awareness;
f) Responsible Business Conduct of Financial Services Providers and Authorised Agents;
g) Protection of Consumer Assets against Fraud and Misuse;
h) Protection of Consumer Data and Privacy;

    i) Complaints Handling and Redress; and
    j) Competition.

These principles have been designed to assist members and other interested economies in their efforts to enhance financial consumer protection. They are voluntary principles, designed to complement, not substitute for, existing international financial principles or guidelines (OECD, 2011).

The enforcement of consumer protection measures can, therefore, directly contribute to increased efficiency of financial intermediation, transparency of financial products and services, and product innovation driven by consumers' demand. Effective consumer protection also facilitates increased penetration of the financial sector, through improved awareness of financial products and services, consumers' rights and obligations, and the advantages of life-long financial planning. On the side of the financial institutions, effective regulation protects them from reputational risks.

5.3 Efforts of the NDIC at Consumer Protection in Nigeria

In line with its mandate and public policy objectives, the NDIC made tremendous efforts over the years to protect consumers of financial services. Consequently, the Corporation has become a visible and well-respected brand in the financial services industry. Some of these efforts include:

5.3.1 Deposit Guarantee

The NDIC provides a limited coverage of all deposit liabilities in DMBs, MFBs and PMBs. The limits were increased from ₦50,000 at inception in 1988 to ₦200,000 in 2006 and later to ₦500,000 in 2010 for depositors of DMBs. The maximum coverage limit for MFBs and PMBs was increased from ₦100,000 in 2006 to ₦200,000 in 2010. However, the coverage limit of PMBs was increased to ₦500,000 in 2016 while deposit insurance coverage was extended to subscribers of mobile money operators in the same year. Furthermore, to encourage sound risk management practices among insured institutions, the Differential Premium Assessment System (DPAS) was adopted in 2007.

To further enhance the effectiveness of the deposit insurance scheme, the Corporation is seeking a reduction in the number of days within which it could reimburse depositors in the event of bank failure from 90 days to 30 days through the proposed amendment of its Act. The proposed NDIC Act CAP N 102 LFN 2012 (repeal and enactment) bill is still before the National Assembly of the Federal Republic of Nigeria at the time of the preparation of this book.

5.3.2 Banking Supervision

The NDIC engages in on-site examination and off-site surveillance of insured banks. It has also created a Special Insured Institutions Department to supervise MFBs and PMBs. In collaboration with the CBN, the Corporation engages in Risk Assets Examination, Risk-Based Supervision, Consolidated Risk-Based Supervision and monitoring of DMBs. Furthermore, in line with the Corporation's public policy objective of promotion of public confidence in the banking industry through consumer protection, the Corporation continues to investigate petitions/complaints that are received from bank customers and other stakeholders.

5.3.3 *Distress Resolution*

In the area of failure resolution, four mechanisms had been applied, namely: Open Bank Assistance, Depositor Reimbursement, Purchase & Assumption and Bridge Bank.

For instance, under the Open Bank Assistance, the Corporation granted accommodation facility of ₦2.3 billion to some banks to resolve their temporary liquidity problems in 1989. Also, seven distressed banks were acquired, restructured and sold to new investors. There was also the take-over of management of 28 banks to safeguard their assets. The thirteen banks that failed to meet the ₦25 billion recapitalisation deadline in 2005 were resolved using Purchase and Assumption, while bridge bank option was used to resolve the problem of three failed banks in 2009.

5.3.4 *Redistributing the Cost of Failures*

In countries like Tunisia and Saudi Arabia where there is no explicit DIS, the cost of protecting depositors often falls on the government. This is not the case in Nigeria, since there is a fully functional DIS that is operated by the NDIC. This has reduced the government's financial obligation for protection, by limiting coverage and providing a mechanism through which healthy institutions may cover all or a portion of the costs associated with resolving failures.

5.3.5 *Promoting Competition in Deposit-Taking Institutions*

In the absence of deposit protection, depositors are likely to prefer using large, well-known institutions that are perceived to be less risky. With the existence of the

DIS in Nigeria, this is minimised as the burden of choice of banks to be patronised, especially by small savers is eased. Also, small and big banks are able to compete on a more level playing field than would have been possible without a DIS.

5.3.6 Contribution to Financial Stability Fund

Following the 2008 crisis in the banking industry, and the institutionalisation of the Financial Stability Fund (FSF), the NDIC initiated a downward review of the premium payable by the banks, and in 2011 reduced the premium base rate from 50 basis points to 40 basis which was further reduced to 35 basis points in 2014.

5.3.7 Development of Framework for the Extension of Deposit Insurance Coverage to Subscribers of Mobile Money Services

As a support for the financial inclusion drive, the NDIC developed a framework for the extension of deposit insurance coverage to Mobile Money Subscribers. Accordingly, the subscribers of MMOs enjoy coverage up to a maximum of ₦500,000 in the event of failure of a bank where the MMO maintains the pool account.

5.3.8 Research and Consumer Surveys

In the quest for continuous depositor protection, the NDIC had conducted various research studies and projects aimed at gathering information and proffering solutions on issues and developments in the financial services sector and the economy as a whole. These studies provide useful information for the creation of consumer protection related policies and drives. Some of the research projects undertaken included:

i.   Automated Teller Machine Frauds: Causes, Extent, Implications and Remedies (2011);
ii. Survey on Financial Literacy in Nigeria (2011);
iii. Collaborative Study on the Framework for Credit Management in Nigerian Banks (2012/2013);
iv. Development of Case Studies on Bank Failure in Nigeria (2015-2017);
v.   Early Warning System of Bank Distress in Nigeria (2013);
vi. Target Fund Ratio Framework (2013); and
vii. Survey on Public Awareness of Deposit Insurance System in Nigeria (2013).

5.3.9 *Consumer Education and Financial Literacy*

NDIC has always made efforts to educate consumers on financial literacy in order to be well informed. These efforts include the introduction of Deposit Insurance System (DIS) curriculum in tertiary institutions, collaboration with other safety-net players in financial literacy, effective public awareness on the activities of the NDIC through publications, participation in international trade fairs, television and radio programmes, amongst others.

5.4   Challenges of NDIC in Consumer Protection

One of the greatest challenges that facing the Corporation is the low-level of public awareness of the DIS. Also, the Fiscal Responsibility Act which requires that 80% of the Corporation's operating surplus should be remitted to the Consolidated Revenue Account of the federation constraints the rapid build-up of the Insurance Fund. Similarly, the long drawn-out litigation by erstwhile shareholders/directors of some closed banks and cumbersome judicial process have also been constraints to effective discharge of the Corporation's mandate, while the poor corporate governance practices of insured institutions constitute a constant risk.

However, the NDIC continues to mitigate these factors by building capacity to ensure the effective and efficient discharge of its mandate, creating innovative ways of enhancing public awareness and sensitisation about DIS, while also ensuring operational readiness at all times. The proposed NDIC Act CAP N 102 LFN 2012 (repeal and enactment) bill, when enacted is expected to address the above challenges.

5.5 Conclusion

Consumers are important recipients of financial products and services. They are also considered unprofessional clients, as they tend to lack sufficient economic, financial and legal knowledge that would ensure equality between the client and the financial institution. Therefore, an effective consumer protection framework consists of three complementary aspects namely: laws and regulations governing relations between service providers and users, which ensures fairness, transparency and recourse rights; effective enforcement mechanism including dispute resolution; and financial literacy and capability, which helps financial services customers to acquire necessary knowledge and skills to manage their finances.

NDIC through its DIS, as an integral part of an effective safety-net framework is committed to strengthening consumer protection, improving consumers' access to financial literacy and raising consumers' financial capabilities.

References

Financial Stability Board (2011). Consumer Finance Protection with Particular Focus on Credit, Basel: Financial Stability Board

Financial Stability Board (2012). Thematic Review on Deposit Insurance Systems, Basel: FSB. Retrieved from: http://www.financialstabilityboard.org/publications/r_120208.pdf

International Association of Deposit Insurers (2017). Annual Report 2016/2017, Basel: IADI. Retrieved from: http://www.iadi.org/en/core-principlesandresearch/publications/annual-reports/

LaBrosse, R. and Mayes, D. (2008). Promoting Financial Stability Through Effective Depositor Protection: The case for explicit limited deposit insurance. InCampbell, A.,Labrosse, R.,Mayes, D. and Singh, D. (eds.), *Deposit Insurance*, pp.1-39, Basingstoke: Palgrave-Macmillan.

Lumpkin, S. (2010). Consumer Protection and Financial Innovation: A Few Basic Propositions, *OECD Journal:* Financial Market Trends, Vol. 2010(1): 1-23

McCharty, I. (1980). Deposit Insurance Theory and Practice. *IMF Economic Review* 27(3): 578–600

Muller, P., Devnani, S., Heys, R. and Suter, J. (2014). Consumer Protection Aspects of Financial Services. *Policy Department A: Economic and Scientific Policy, 1-141*

Organisation for Economic Co-operation and Development (2011). G20 High-Level Principles on Financial Consumer Protection, Paris: OECD

Pennacchi, G. G. (2009). Deposit Insurance. Being paper prepared for AEI Conference on Private Markets and Public Insurance Programs, March

United Nations Conference on Trade and Development, UNCTAD (2016). Manual on Consumer Protection. United Nations Publication UNCTAD/WEB/DITC/CLP/2016/1, United Nations: UNCTAD

William Allen and Geoffrey Wood, (2006). Defining and Achieving Financial   Stability, *Journal of Financial Stability*, 2(2): 152-172

6

STRATEGIES FOR ADDRESSING CUSTOMER COMPLAINTS IN BANKS[6]

6.0   Introduction

Ever since the deregulation of the banking system, following the introduction of the structural adjustment programme (SAP) in 1986, the number of banks and bank branches have increased tremendously. Though the numbers were trimmed in response to the 2004 bank recapitalisation, they still remained significant particularly in terms of branches. We also now have both 'old' and 'new' generation banks, reflecting their pre- or post-reform existence. The growth in banks and the ensuing competition in the variety of financial products that are introduced, have not been matched with the growth and quality of manpower to serve the industry. In consequence, there has been a significant decline in

---

6   Original version of this paper was presented at the 2-day Workshop organised by CIBN between November 15 and 16, 2011 at Sheraton Hotels, Ikeja,, Lagos.

the quality of service delivery and declining integrity exhibited by the bank personnel. These failures may find expression in such issues as impoliteness of staff, unnecessary delays in service delivery, excessive charges and hidden fees, fraud on the part of bank employees, all of which could negatively impact on the reputation of a bank and the banking industry at large.

With these developments, the challenge of sustaining the customer confidence and meeting their expectations by commercial banks have become complex. The responsibility of handling customer expectations and complaints and the overall protection of customer deposits lie with the NDIC as the deposit insurer. The role of the NDIC in protecting the customer and responding promptly to complaints is critical in ensuring that potential loss of confidence does not degenerate into financial systemic crisis that can cause a run on banks. In response, the NDIC has developed strategies and mechanisms for maintaining customer confidence by receiving and handling customer complaints timely.

In the rest of the chapter we delve into the customer expectations, the causes of customer complaints, attempts at addressing such customer complaints, and the various measures for preventing and controlling customer complaints in Nigerian banks. The last section concludes the chapter.

6.1 Customer Expectations in Banks

A dissatisfied customer is unlikely to continue a relationship with a bank and his/her experience could be the reason a potential new customer might be discouraged from opening a new bank account. The EFInA report (EFInA A2F. 2016) suggested customer dissatisfaction as one of the reasons the percentage of adults with a bank account in Nigeria was as low as 38.3% in the period under reference. Customers are major stakeholders in banking business, as deposits form the biggest liabilities on a bank's balance sheet. The Board and Management of the banks should therefore be alert to the various expectations of customers in designing new products and creating innovative incentives that not only retain existing customers, but also attract new customers. Shammout and Haddad (2014) have identified areas of service quality customers expect to receive from their banks. These include:

i) Credibility and trustworthiness of the bank.

ii) Responsiveness of the bank to perform services accurately and in a timely manner.

iii) Security of funds held by the bank.

iv) Understanding and adapting to the clients' needs to offer tailored services to them.

v) Accessibility of the banking institution, either by proximity of the physical location or online.

vi) Competence in skills and knowledge of bank employees.

vii) Courtesy when dealing with customers, treating them with respect and appreciation.

viii) Reliability of the bank to consistently perform services efficiently without any delays.

ix) Communicating to the customers of risks, providing updates and all pertinent information relating to their accounts in a timely manner.

The need to design policies that adapt to customer expectations cannot be overemphasised, especially in

Nigerian banks. Customers are not only depositors, but creditors, contractors, shareholders and other stakeholders. The inability to manage customers' expectations coupled with the serious corporate governance issues explain, in large part, the high frequency of complaints amongst bank customers in Nigeria.

6.2   Causes of Customer Complaints in Nigeria Banks

The nature of customer complaints in banks take different forms, ranging from service-related complaints to issues of integrity and accountability as well as those arising from poor management. Some of the reasons responsible for customer complaints include:

- Poor Services: The main link between a bank and its customers is the service it renders. The services need to be of high quality in order to meet the standards and expectations of customers. Where the quality of service is poor and falls short of expectations of customers, complaints are bound to occur. Examples of poor services offered by Nigerian banks are:
- long waiting time to be attended to in the banking halls;
- limited branch network in respect of some banks;
- limited number of ATM machines and incessant network failures;
- delays in dealing with funds transfer;
- lack of courtesy by teller officers and receptionists;
- cumbersome loan procedures; and
- limited number of products.

- High Bank Tariffs/Charges: Banks derive their income from interest charges as well as commissions and other charges. However, outrageous tariffs/charges could lead to complaints by customers. Examples of these situations include high maintenance fees, overdraft charges, interest charges on loans, administrative charges and indiscriminate charges on customer account, etc.

- Frauds and Forgeries: Frauds and forgeries perpetrated on customers' accounts is a ground for complaints. Examples include deliberate refusal to post actual amounts of lodgements into customers' accounts, cheque kiting, ATM frauds, among others.

- Bank Distress/Failure: A bank that has fallen into distress makes withdrawals of deposits by their customers difficult. Their cheques/drafts may not be honoured by people or other banks, thereby causing frustration and sometimes, loss of money to their customers.

- Information Asymmetry: Adequate disclosure to stakeholders on issues that affect them seems to be taken for granted, especially in this jurisdiction. Banks often effect changes on charges/commissions for services without adequately informing customers. Some customers get to know certain changes regarding the services rendered by the banks only at the point of enjoying them and that can cause disaffection and could be a basis for complaints.

Other complaints include weak internal controls leading to accounting errors; cumbersome/malfunction/non-compliance of processes, procedures and benchmarks; lack of information on the availability of banking products; gaps in expected versus actual services rendered, etc. (Khushhali Bank, 2008).

6.3 Regulatory Attempts at Addressing Customer Complaints in Banks

Ideally, the responsibility of handling customer complaints should be with the banks. But in Nigerian context, small savers who are most vulnerable to some unwholesome practices of banks are victimised. This is because banks traditionally focus on their high net-worth clients and tend to ignore the small scale depositors who actually account for the larger population of banks customers. But it is the relatively small percentage of the high net-worth clients who account for the bulk of the deposit liability of banks. To prevent small depositors from being marginalised and losing confidence in the banking system, regulatory authorities in collaboration with operators, have instituted procedures for minimising and resolving customer complaints when they occur. Some of these include:

a. Prompt Supervisory Intervention which includes continuous surveillance on the banks to ensure that they remain sound and render quality services to the satisfaction and expectations of customers. Even though there has been a serious challenge of data integrity in the banking system, the NDIC alertness to supervision and interventions have averted the failures of some banks, thus minimising what would have been severe consequences for the customers of the affected banks. A case in point was the intervention in respect of some eight distressed banks in 2010, three of which were converted into bridge banks and sold to Asset Management Corporation of Nigeria (AMCON).

b. Consumer Protection Framework: In 2016, the CBN in its circular, *CPD/DIR/GEN/CPF/03/004* released its Consumer Protection Framework aimed at guaranteeing high standards of customer service delivery, market discipline and ensuring that consumers are treated fairly by financial institutions. The objectives of the framework include, protecting consumers' assets; timely complaints; handling dispute resolution; effective risk management frameworks established by operators; empowering consumers with knowledge and information on their rights; promotion of professionalism and ethics.

c. Establishment of a Consumer Protection Department by CBN. A customer protection department was set up in response to the series of daily complaints the CBN was receiving against the banks and other financial institutions. The department attends to complaints and resolves issues that can be resolved at the desk level and refer others to the appropriate channels that can handle them.

d. Establishment of the NDIC Help Desk. A customer help desk was established by the NDIC in response to the numerous complaints it receives against both existing and failed banks. The desk is a toll-free line and has proven to be a worthwhile idea as a lot of bank customer complaints have been received and resolved. A total of 309 and 595 calls were received through the help desk in 2016 and 2017, respectively. The complaints centred mainly on deposit pay-out for failed DMBs and closed MFBs, suspension of payments by Agent Banks, status of shareholders of DMBs in-liquidation as well as disparity in depositors' statement of accounts. Also, a total of 2,892 e-mails were received at the help desk in 2017. Most of the e-mails were complaints and petitions against DMBs, PMBs and MFBs. All the aforementioned complaints were forwarded to the relevant Departments for investigations and feedbacks.

e. Establishment of Ethics and Professionalism Sub-Committee of Bankers' Committee. Through the collaborative efforts of regulatory/supervisory authorities and banks, the Sub-committee of Bankers' Committee on Ethics and Professionalism was set up to attend to both customer complaints and banks as well.

6.4   Strategies for the Resolution of Customer Complaints in Banks

As already highlighted, excellent customer service should be the number one objective of banks. Where grievances exist, banks should ensure adequate measures are in place to attend to and resolve customers' complaints. This task requires concerted effort from top management to institute a customer-centric culture to build trust that endears banks to customers. Some effective strategies for creating such a customer-centric culture in banks include network building, co-creation and personalisation (Ernst & Young, 2014). This simply means banks need to anticipate what the customer requires, match those needs with what the bank can provide and bring these solutions to the doorstep of the customer. While this may seem straightforward, Nigerian banks have historically failed to provide a variety of services to meet the demands of the customers; instead all banks have tended to provide the same services wrapped in different names. Only the truly enterprising banks reap the rewards of true customer-centric banking.

To ensure high consumer confidence in the sector, the regulators have encouraged the following actions by banks:

a. Reduced Charges and Tariffs: Although this may depend on exogenous factors such as the prevailing monetary policy rate and business environment, banks should make efforts to avoid exorbitant administrative charges that could put more burden on, their credit customers.

b. Strengthening of Customer Care Desk: The customer care desks that attend to customers' enquiries and other basic needs, should be strengthened to enable them attend to issues beyond complaints on ATM, checking of account balances, issuance of cheque books, to include attending to any other complaints that customers might have against the bank and channelling same to the appropriate unit/section for resolution.

c. Improved IT Infrastructure: IT as the backbone that drives the operations of banks, needs to be in good shape at all times for complaints from customers to be managed and controlled effectively. Such issues include bank network failures for which the IT could provide the required back-up to ensure seamless operations, when there are disruptions on the main infrastructural facility.

d. Continuous Customer Education: The need to keep customers informed about changes and new products and services in the banks cannot be overemphasised. This can be done through advertisements and announcements in the print and electronic media, mobile phones, etc.

e. Human Capacity Development: Customer complaints arising from poor service delivery could be as a result of inadequate knowledge and skills on the part of the staff to deliver on the job. Adequate training and retraining could empower employees to improve on service delivery, which could ensure effective management and control of customer complaint.

f. Establishment of a Financial Ombudsman: Since the activities of the Nigerian Consumer Protection Council seems not to have adequately satisfied the needs of customers in the financial services industry, there is the need to establish a Financial Ombudsman Scheme in the country. A financial ombudsman is a scheme that could be set up by government with the objective of enabling the resolution of complaints relating to certain services rendered by banks and to facilitate the satisfaction or settlement of such complaints. As of the time of this publication, a bill on Financial Ombudsman was before the National Assembly. NDIC continues to lobby the National Assembly to expedite its passage into law before the end of the 8th Assembly. When enacted, it will help to address the challenges of protection of consumers of financial services as well as protect the integrity of the financial system. In other jurisdictions such as United States and India, the scheme is under the Reserve Bank. With such a scheme in place, complaints against the banks by their customers could be expeditiously addressed.

g. Strengthening of Corporate Governance in Banks: Poor corporate governance has been responsible for the distressed situations some banks have found themselves. The distressed condition could cause rendition of poor service by the affected banks. When sound corporate governance is entrenched in banks, complaints arising from the inability of the banks to deliver to their customers could be prevented and controlled. In this regard, it is to be noted that the CBN had since 2006, following the banking sector consolidation, issued a Code of Corporate Governance that is expected to guide the behaviour of management for all banks.

6.5 Conclusion

Continuous and unresolved complaints against banks will threaten confidence, not only in the affected banks, but the entire system at large. Banks are therefore advised to take prompt steps to address customer complaints seriously. Banks should, in this regard, consider the establishment of a complaint resolution mechanism that not only oversees the work of their customer relation desks, but also establishes a Complaints Resolution Database that serves the following functions: catalogues and classifies complaints, records complaints settlement time and manages follow-up procedures to ensure customers are completely satisfied. This database can be the basis of a framework used to pre-empt service delivery failures in the future.

The salient points to remember by banks, according to the Khushhali Bank Limited (2008) are: customer complaints should be tools to address shortcomings; customers should be treated fairly with the highest professional standards; customers are fully informed of avenues to escalate their complaints if they are not fully satisfied; and employees should work in good faith in the interest of the customers.

The regulatory/supervisory authorities, on their part, will continue to strengthen the supervisory framework so as to ensure that the system remains safe and sound for quality services to be rendered to bank customers at all times.

References

Consumer Protection Framework (2016) Central Bank of Nigeria Circular: *CPD/DIR/GEN/CPF/03/004*

Enhancing Financial Innovation and Access (EFInA) Access to Finance Survey 2016

Ernst & Young and Efma Global Survey Report (2014). Global Survey Report: Looking at the bank from the customer's point of view

Khushhali Bank Limited (2008). Customers Complaints Handling Policy & Procedures

Shammout, M. Z. & Haddad, S. I. (2014) The Impact of Complaints' Handling on Customer Satisfaction: Empirical Study on Commercial Banks' Clients in Jordan. *International Business Research*, Vol. 7, No. 11, pp. 203-220

7

EMERGING ISSUES IN CORPORATE GOVERNANCE[7]

7.0 Introduction

Corporate governance has been described by the Organisation for Economic Co-operation and Development (OECD) as a set of structured relationships between a company's Board, its shareholders, and other stakeholders through which the objectives and monitoring performance are determined (OECD, 1999). In general, Boards are established to provide oversight functions that give direction and provide control to the managers of an organisation. The inner workings of the Boards provide strict rules and procedures that guide the responsibilities of directors, who are themselves appointed on their known competencies and relevant professional and technical exposure. In spite of the fact that corporations might be supervised by an all-star Board, corporate scandals and failures do occur (Hansell, 2003). Even though Ingley and Van der Walt (2005) had reported that corporate

---

7   Original version of this paper was delivered at the CBN/FITC Continuous Education Programme for Directors of Banks, October 15, 2014.

governance reform had gained momentum on a worldwide scale, the failure of corporate governance amply demonstrated in the global financial-crisis of 2007 to 2009 emphasised the urgency of this reform.

In the banking industry in Nigeria, the 2009 CBN and NDIC special examination of the 24 banks in operation revealed that 10 banks were critically distressed, mainly as a result of poor corporate governance practices. Directors, regulators, shareholders, policy makers and the general public need to, therefore, pay greater attention to the issue of corporate governance in their organisations, whether public or private.

7.1 Legislations Guiding Responsibilities and Liabilities of Directors

Globally, several legislations provide for directors' duties and liabilities. In the United Kingdom, some of the legislations include the UK Companies Acts 2006, and the UK Financial Services Act 1986. In the United States, they include the Dodd-Frank Wall Street Reform, Consumer Protection Act and Sarbanes Oxley Act. The first Code of Best Practices for Public Companies operating in Nigeria was published in 2003 and reviewed in 2009, amidst the global economic crisis. Other legislations for the financial sector include the Companies and Allied Matters Act, the Nigerian Deposit Insurance Corporation Act 2006, (NDIC Act), the Central Bank of Nigeria Act 2007 (CBN Act), and the Banks and other Financial Institutions Act 1991 (BOFIA).

The 2003 Code asserts that corporate governance serves as a guide to facilitate sound corporate practices and behaviour. The Code is seen as a dynamic document that defines the minimum standards of corporate governance expected particularly of public companies with listed securities. The Code also states that the responsibility for ensuring compliance with or observance of the principles and provisions of the Code rests primarily on the Board of Directors. Institutional shareholders are, however, expected to familiarise themselves with the letter and spirit of the Code and encourage or whenever necessary, demand compliance by their companies.

Exercising its powers, the CBN issued a Code of Corporate Governance for Banks and Other Financial Institutions in August 2003, revised in 2006 and 2014. Similarly, SEC issued the Code of Corporate Governance for Publicly Quoted Companies in 2003 and revised in 2009. Further to this, the Financial Reporting Council (FRC) of Nigeria is empowered by FRC Act 2011 to give guidance on issues relating to corporate governance and to ensure good corporate governance practices in the public and private sectors of the Nigerian economy. The FRC has developed a national code of corporate governance that provides a minimum standard expected of all organisations. The Code as of the time of this publication was undergoing public hearing to ensure wide stakeholder acceptability when released. It will serve as a handbook to the various sector regulators.

7.2   Responsibilities of Directors

Blair and Stout (1999), analyse US Corporate Law and argue that although it may be most efficient to have directors elected by shareholders, their fundamental responsibility is with the firm itself. Hence, the principal-agent representation of the corporation is at odds with the legal description of the firm as a separate entity. This means the shareholders cannot formally be taken as principals. On the contrary, the Board of Directors itself is better conceived as representing the top of the corporate hierarchy, whose fundamental role is to mediate between all corporate stakeholders in situations where stakeholders' interests do not necessarily coincide (Kostant, 1999).

A broader view of directors' responsibilities is likely to lead to inclusion of strategic tasks such as policy formulation and determining the company's strategic objectives. These roles imply responsibility for the appointment of senior management, who direct the daily operations of the company and account for its activities at regular intervals to shareholders and constant monitoring of the firm's progress towards the attainment of the set targets, including attention paid to the welfare and safety of employees at workplace. The central objective here is to enhance stakeholders'/ shareholders' value while minimising conflicts of interests within the company.

7.3 The Liabilities of Directors

The liabilities of a director will crystallise if he/she contravenes the Code of Corporate Governance guiding the operations of the industry. The UK revised Company Law of 2006 indicates that the liability as a director can be forever, even to cover his/her estate.

In Nigeria, there is no limit on directors' liabilities under the Nigerian law, save for where CAMA or any other applicable rules/laws prescribe particular punishments. Where a company prefers that a director's liability be limited, it is required to state so in its memorandum. (Section 279 (9)) of CAMA provides that a duty imposed by the company on any given director shall be enforceable against the director by the company. The Act also makes provisions for others to bring actions on behalf of the company in the event the action is of the interest of the director.

The point here is, effective director recruitment and

retention efforts include an organised response to anxieties concerning individual liability exposure. An obvious step is to assure availability of comprehensive insurance and indemnification coverage for board members. More substantive responses relate to: assuring that decision-making processes satisfy business judgment rule requirements; oversight processes are substantive and based on effective information reporting systems; and that directors are trained to recognise and respond to warning and red flags of risk.

In addition, directors' quest to engage a company's business to yield optimum returns must take cognizance of market challenges as to how to handle the many market rumours, indirect feedback and information relevant to corporate reputation that inevitably come across director's desk. One way that outside directors can reduce the already low likelihood of bearing personal liability is, they should be aware that their risk increases when their company makes a public offering of shares.

7.4 Emerging issues in Corporate Governance

Due to the positive effect of globalisation in the contemporary business landscape, large corporations have benefitted from capital market integration. This development has meant separating investors or wealth owners from the control of the firms in which they invest. In other words, investors in the western jurisdictions can own large stakes in African corporations, and vice versa without having to travel to the investing environments. Skilled labour can also be outsourced across borders, making the entire world a global village. One of the downsides of free-flowing of investment funds across jurisdictions is that the investors may not always be able to verify the integrity of agents and managers of their corporations who influence the firm's decisions, and this may act to the detriment of the outside investors.

A few models have emerged to handle this contemporary issue. One is the 'Anglo-American shareholder governance model', commonly referred to as the 'principal-agent' model, which regards the central problem of corporate governance as self-interested managerial behaviour, when the agent does not share the principal's objectives (Shleifer & Vishny, 1997; Gupta, Otley & Young, 2008). In this respect, advocates of the Anglo-American governance model identify the need to provide the outside investors with adequate protection through a formal rule-based approach.

The second model is the 'stakeholder approach' (Freeman, 1984; Jones, 1995; Sikka, 2008; and Fassin, 2009). This model adopts a wider objective function of the firm as more equitable and more socially efficient, compared to the 'principal-agent' or shareholder's wealth. It is argued in this model that, in addition to the investing shareholders, the well-being of other stakeholder groups such as employees, consumers, suppliers, customers, creditors, other service providers, and even the local community, who have a long-term association with the organisation and therefore, a stake in its long-term success, should be recognised.

A synthesis of these two models have guided reforms in the emerging corporate governance issues which serves as a guide in the presentation of the remaining sections of this chapter which focus on Board selection, balance, size, and risk management, the way forward and conclusion.

7.4.1 Board Selection

The best practice is to employ an explicit competency-based selection process.

The aim is to achieve an optimal board membership

-mix that not only meets regulatory and governmental expectations, but that also makes the board effective and productive. The selection should take account of diversity of membership in terms of experience, expertise, skill sets, perspectives and gender. Gender becomes an issue here as 50% of the global population is women but only 10% are board members.

7.4.2 Board Balance

Generally, independent directors aid in balancing the interests of the shareholders, employees and creditors. This balancing role is particularly important in situations where conflicts arise between the interests of the executive directors and the shareholders. The presence of independent directors serves to bring about impartiality in the Board as a whole. On balance, independent directors aid in strengthening the leadership qualities of the Board. In Ghana, Abor and Adjasi (2007) found that the presence of external independent directors on the Board team enhances corporate competitiveness and provides new strategic outlook.

While Board independence is considered a necessary condition for effective monitoring, there is a growing recognition that the Board quality is important for governance (Sarkar, 2009). In Nigeria, Sanda *et al* (2008) found that foreign managers perform better than their local counterparts.

The Nigerian Code does not specifically state the proportion of independent directors to executive directors in the composition of the Board (Anglo-American model), though director independence is becoming more evident internationally (McCabe & Nowak, 2008). The Board should however be balanced with the majority of directors being non-executive (NEDs) and independent. Independent directors should be knowledgeable about the business and possess qualities of objectivity, experience, insight, and character.

7.4.3 Board Size

The size of the Board should be large enough to include a diversity of the competencies it needs to exercise its responsibilities, but small enough to engage everyone in active discussion, make timely decisions, and bond together as a team. The Nigerian corporate governance regime is characterised by a combination of statutory framework and subsidiary legislation enacted by the relevant regulatory authorities. These laws are divided into two categories: the general laws and the sector-specific laws. The Companies and Allied Matters Act (CAMA) is the main statute delimiting the general framework for the Nigerian Corporate Governance regime, while the CBN Code is sector specific, which is consistent with best practice. The Code places a lot of premium on the independence of the Board. It prescribes a minimum and maximum Board size of five and twenty directors, respectively with greater number of non-executive directors, two of whom must be independent directors.

7.4.4 Risk Management

The corporate governance aspect of risk management remains a challenge in a number of banks as witnessed in the widespread failure of risk management in global banks. The Board should understand risk management and understand that it is not enough to keep risk register while being aware that, not all risks are quantifiable. It should be capable of identifying the key risks in their business, understand where the cash is and how it is expended, appreciate the impact of bad debts/NPLs, and appreciate the financial impact of risks that form potential loss to the business. For proper risk management, the Board should assume nothing, believe nobody but check everything. The dictum should be "We never invest in a business we do not understand".

Taking the Nigerian banking industry as a case in point, the special audit of twenty-four banks by the CBN/NDIC in 2009 revealed several corporate governance breaches. This unearthed several instances of self-serving Boards and Management, insider dealings and Board squabbles, uneven concentration of Board power, lack of Board commitment to establishing best practices and a great problem of competence, where inexperienced/unskilled members were present on the Boards. There was also inadequate succession planning, poor risk management policies, inadequate minority shareholder protection, lack of 'whistle-blowing' policies/mechanisms, insufficient shareholder activism (institutional and individual shareholders), as well as weak supervision.

Further to this, an examination of fifteen banks conducted by the CBN/NDIC in July 2014, revealed some corporate governance breaches by Nigerian banks, including inadequate loan loss provisions, operation of ambiguous organisational reporting structure which goes against the principle of unity of command and which has the potential of undermining and diluting the authority of the Managing Director/Chief Executive Officer, as well as the Executive Management. Some Boards did not participate actively in exercising oversight running of their banks. There was also high incidence of fraud cases by banks staff, indicating weak internal controls and poor operational risk management practices, while some banks did not have capital plans to support their strategic intents. There were several breaches of non-executive directors' remuneration by some banks contrary to Section 5.3.9 of the Code of Corporate Governance, as well as breach of insider-related facilities as a percentage of their respective paid-up capital, contrary to the provision of the CBN circular Ref no. *BSD/09/2004* dated 16th July, 2004.

The identified issues led to several reforms and re-regulation of the banking sector, which includes the following:

a. instituting a common financial year end for all banks;

b. adoption of framework for consolidated supervision;

c. issuance of guidelines for holding companies (HOLDCO);

d. regulation on margin lending;

e. full adoption of IFRS, mandated by 2012 and new detailed minimum reporting requirement for banks;

f. restricting the tenure of banks CEOs and Board members to a maximum of 10 years;

g. Bankers' Committee reinvigorated for advocacy of economic development;

h. The requirement for independence and use of external auditors; and

i. The release of circular on Code of Corporate Governance for banks and discount houses in Nigeria by the CBN.

The cyclical nature of economic and financial crises indicate that such crises could still occur, but that the impact can be minimised by keeping the lessons learnt from recent episodes at the back of our minds, and therefore being careful of similar pitfalls going forward. In doing that, Board members must indeed learn these pertinent lessons, and become more focused, more knowledgeable, more informed and committed. Boards should remain alert to the dangers of a gradual build-up of NPLs, and loan concentration in some sectors, such as the energy sector, and address them proactively.

7.5 The Way Forward

Abraham Lincoln stated that "We must plan for the future because those who stay in the present will remain in the past" (1862). This quotation shows the importance of extrapolating from the past to create better possibilities for the future. Situating this in the context of corporate governance in Nigeria will ensure continued stability in institutions. Corporate governance must always remain an issue of prime importance. The following issues must be addressed by banks and their Boards to ensure adequate corporate governance practices, as well as prevent or reduce the possibility of crises in our institutions.

i. Implementation of guidelines and policies approved by the Board based on a robust risk management framework of the bank.

ii. Fair and adequate staff compensation.

iii. Effective staff development.

iv. Practice of good Corporate Social Responsibility (CSR): Evidence from the audit of citizens reveal a poor perception of the banks in terms of their social and economic impacts. Generally, measurement of social cost and benefits would assist a bank to put itself on the path of sustainable growth and viability. The Board should be able to evaluate how satisfactorily their banks have discharged their CSRs. How are the

Boards responding to poor perception by customers/ citizens? More attention should be paid to this issue.

v. Diversity: Companies that want to attract the best talent must think about work friendly environment. Premium must be placed on fair treatment of gender issues and recognising the need for more flexible working hours which makes work more productive and family friendly.

vi. Good values/ethics at the Board level must be emphasised, promoting the culture of integrity, professionalism, fairness and caring. Adequate policies must be put in place to address the issues of stealing and fraud while promoting honesty and compassion. The Boards must also become effective in driving consumer education and consumer protection initiatives so as to mitigate reputational risks.

vii. Strategy is of utmost importance. The Board should appreciate that strategy drives finance and not otherwise; so the Board should decide on the appropriate growth model. For instance, should it be "a build model – organic growth or buy model – such as Mergers and Acquisition (M & A) or borrow model?" The Board should be able to provide directions on appropriate business model, time-relevance of the business model given the dynamics of banking business, and the actions of competitors.

viii. Environmental Management/Sustainability issues. In Nigeria, banks have resolved through the Bankers Committee, to embrace sustainable banking practices as it is becoming a new trend in today's modern banking business (see Chapter 5). It is about preserving the environment and biodiversity for future generations and about being cautious with natural resources and climate. The importance of sustainable banking is that, for a bank to develop commercially, it has to look at the big picture and act in ways that benefit the economy, society and the environment.

Taken together, it is important for the Board to appreciate that hope is not strategy. The Boards should be well involved in strategy formulation and execution for banks to survive profitably and be on a sustainable basis. For the individual, there are some critical information that needs to be obtained before joining a Board, given the enormity of responsibilities and liabilities of a director. It will be of importance to any interested individual that is considering of becoming a director or a Board, to seek for information on the company's values/culture; risk assessment reports, external auditor's management letters as well as management accounts. Pending litigation – which determines contingent liabilities are also relevant, as are tax payment/obligation records, and any regulatory issues. The profile of other directors/ top management and the strategy report will all give a clue on the focus and strategic stance of the firm, while reports on any conflict of interest as well as on frauds will serve as red flags to look out for.

7.6 Conclusion

The fact remains that good governance flows from probity, honesty and being ethical in management conduct, together with a value system that promotes trust.

Nigeria modelled its corporate governance framework largely from the UK's, and it is time the largest economy in Africa (Nigeria) prepares to build a better role on the world stage as a potential global trading nation. Recent visits of world leaders to Nigeria is a pointer to the fact that the strength of businesses is critical to future success. Nigerian banks and other companies are hard working and responsible, investing in employees' skills, competing in business creativity and innovation, knowing that this is the way to succeed in the long term. Therefore, a strong and effective system of corporate governance which encourages businesses to take the right long-term decisions, is key to that success. Nigeria must continue to reform its system of corporate governance in line with the best practice to retain her competitive edge. To be good for long-term business, Nigeria should set out a range of legislative and business-led measures, which will improve corporate governance and give workers and investors a stronger voice to those outside the boardroom, and businesses culture would be strengthened to take the right long-term decisions that would help to restore public trust. One of the best ways to maintain business reputation is regular update of the corporate governance framework.

References

Abor, J. and Adjasi, C. K. D. (2007). Corporate governance and the small and medium enterprises sector: Theory and implications. *Corporate Governance*, 7(2), 12

Blair, M. M. and Stout, L. A. (1999). A team production theory of corporate law. *Virginia Law Review*, 85(2), 247-328

BOFIA Act 1991 (As Amended in 1997, 1998, 1999 & 2002)

CBN circular Ref no. *BSD/09/2004* dated 16th July, 2004

Freeman, R. E. (1984). *Strategic Management: A Stakeholder Approach*. Pitman, Boston

Gilson, R. (2006). Controlling shareholders and corporate governance: complicating the comparative taxonomy. *Harvard Law Review* 119, 1641–1679

Hansell, C. (2003). What Directors Need to Know: *Corporate Governance*. Toronto: Thomson Carswell

Ingley, C. and Van der Walt, N. (2005). Do board processes influence director and board performance? Statutory and performance implications. *Corporate Governance*, 13 (5)

Konstant, P. (1999). Exit, voice and loyalty in the course of corporate governance and counsel's changing role course of corporate governance and counsel's changing role. *Journal of Socio Economics*, 28(3), 203-214

La Porta, R., Lopez-de-Silanes, F. and Shleifer, A. (1999). Corporate ownership around the world. *Journal of Finance*, 54(2), 471-518

McCabe, M. and Nowak, M. (2008). The independent director on the board of company directors. *Managerial Auditing Journal*, 23(6), 545-566

NDIC (2006). NDIC Acts 2006

Organization of Economic Co-operation and Development (OECD) (1999). *Principles of Corporate Governance*, OECD, Paris

Shleifer, A. and Vishny, R.W. (1997). A survey of corporate governance. *Journal of Finance*, 52, 737-83.

Sarkar, J. (2009). Board Independence & Corporate Governance in India: recent trends & challenges ahead. *The Indian Journal of Industrial Relations*, 44(4)

Sanda, A. U., Garba, T. and Mikailu, A. S. (2008). Board independence and firm financial performance: evidence from Nigeria. Centre for the Study of African Economies (CSAE) Conference 2008 titled Economic Development in Africa at St Catherine's College, University of Oxford, Oxford

8

THE POTENTIAL ROLE OF CORPORATE SOCIAL RESPONSIBILITY IN POVERTY REDUCTION AND ECONOMIC DEVELOPMENT IN NIGERIA[8]

8.0   Introduction

Corporate Social Responsibility (CSR) is a complex and multidimensional organisational phenomenon. It is often conceptualised as the scope for and the ways in which an organisation is consciously responsible for its actions and non-actions, and their impact on its stakeholders. It represents not just a change to the commercial setting in which individual companies operate, but also a pragmatic response of a company to its consumers and society. It is increasingly being understood as a means by which companies may endeavour to achieve a balance between their efforts to generate profits and the societies that they impact in

---

8   Original version of this paper was a Keynote address delivered at the National Conference on the Role of Corporate Social Responsibility in Poverty Reduction and Economic Development in Nigeria, 2011.

these efforts. Such areas of concern for the corporate self-regulation or as demanded by national laws may cover ecological and social activities such as education, health and other social programmes in a community in which the business operates.

The potential role of CSR in poverty reduction and promotion of economic development depends on the kind of development that a particular country aspires to have. It may be useful to begin with a distinction between two visions of development: modernisation and human development. The primary objective of modernisation is the establishment of an industrial economy and the expansion of its productive capacity. In most parts of the developing world, modernisation projects have typically resulted in extreme unevenness in outcomes, with a modern technologically advanced core corporate economy, co-existing with a vast non-corporate periphery. The criticisms of this paradigm are well-known, and they constitute the basis of human development paradigm.

As distinct from modernisation, human development focuses on people rather than on production as its objective. It is concerned primarily with the reduction of human deprivation, the creation of human capabilities and unleashing "processes that enlarge people's choices" (Ivanov and Peleah, 2008).

This chapter discusses corporate social responsibility and its core principles, convergence of corporate social responsibility and corporate governance, role of development agencies and corporate social responsibility, NDIC's corporate responsibility experiences and conclusion.

8.1 Core Principles of Corporate Social Responsibility

Elkington's (1998) "triple bottom line" is one of the best-known models that seeks to marry the concern for society and the environment with the profit motive in an organisation. In this model, CSR emphasises three responsibilities of a company: social, economic and environmental. The implementation of these responsibilities are necessary to ensure economic prosperity, environmental quality and social justice. These responsibilities are in addition to the legal, ethical and discretionary expectations that a community or society may have for a business organisation at a given time (Carroll, 1999). Another strong argument in the recent CSR practice literature relates to stakeholders engagement in CSR performance to enable them deal with their external environment effectively (Freeman and Reed, 1983).

Arising from the above, CSR practices may be grouped into four major categories:

- The society expects companies to contribute to building better societies and therefore incorporate social concerns into their core strategies as well as consider the full scope of their impact on societies. More particularly, this principle requires companies to implement fair wage policies, uphold human rights, fair trade and ethical issues, produce safe products and cooperate in the network of companies and communities.

- The economic principle emphasises company's efficiency in producing goods without compromising social and environmental values. This principle denotes that, along with their responses to the financial expectations of their shareholders, companies should focus on the economic well-being of the society as a whole.

- The environmental states that the companies should not harm the environment in order to maximise profits, and that companies should have a strong role in repairing environmental damage caused by their exploitation of natural resources.

- The stakeholder approach to CSR practice holds companies responsible for considering the legitimate interests of their stakeholders.

These principles are the drivers of the sources of different CSR practices and hence, important factors for initiating any strategies for developing CSR practices. These principles are used broadly within different segments of government, business and the academic world. The principles are considered to be the cornerstone for the development of socially responsible corporate culture. These CSR principles are now acknowledged by standardisation regimes, global business societies, civil societies and nation states. The main focus of CSR is that companies should be committed to 'contribute to sustainable economic development – working with employees, their families, the local community and society at large to improve the quality of life, in a way that is also good for business.'

8.2 Convergence of CSR and Corporate Governance

Corporate governance and corporate social responsibility have become hard to distinguish in the global economic landscape. Their convergence in the face of regulatory, business, and social changes in transnational markets has evoked debate and controversy over both the potential and limitations of corporate accountability mechanisms. Recently, scholars and practitioners in many fields have looked beyond their traditional perceptions to explore how synthesising governance and responsibility may affect existing practices in business and social advocacy.

The hybridisation between corporate governance and corporate social responsibility is typically viewed by the mainstream in the business community and in the CSR movement as an innovative process that holds promise for markets as well as the society. Paul *et al* (1999) expressed concern regarding the potential policy outcomes of this process from both a business and social change perspective. Business advocates often fear that dedicating considerable efforts to meeting social and environmental demands will distract managers from focusing on financial wealth creation and serving the interests of investors. Michael (2001) agreed with Nobel Prize winner, Milton Friedman that, "the social responsibility of business is to increase its profits," and that the more corporate governance is preoccupied by non-business activities, the less it will fulfil its designated role.

On the other hand, CSR-sceptics who seek public policies aimed at achieving economic justice have serious reservations about the direction the stakeholder movement is taking. They argue that, if CSR becomes preoccupied with business decision-making, the movement-already critiqued as one that essentially helps corporations to market themselves more effectively, will become even more corporate-friendly and less effective in promoting economic justice. A growing voice within the research literature takes a more intricate approach to this policy debate. This approach acknowledges all of the limitations mentioned above, but chooses to pursue the potential of corporate governance, CSR, and their interaction in reconstructing markets. The proponents of this approach often share many of the concerns expressed by the CSR-sceptics but are captivated by the opportunity of turning companies into semi-public entities and creating a more democratic business environment via corporate social responsibility. The two areas most likely to face the long-term challenges highlighted by this policy debate are business regulation and social change advocacy.

In a public atmosphere that places emphasis on corporate ethics and social responsibility, the regulation of business and finance may undergo changes that would mitigate some of the current focus on profit maximisation. The current wave of meta-regulation and "soft" law may inevitably shift more efforts from the legislature to public coalitions, NGOs, investment groups, and other social players. This shift may also encourage administrative agencies to extend their collaboration with the private sector and further engage in sentencing guidelines and incentives for self-enforcement.

Kent (2007) suggested that substantively, business regulation-whether "hard" or "soft"- is likely to become socially-conscious and absorb some of the "Triple Bottom Line" practices that increasingly link business with sustainability. Voluntary mechanisms may become mandatory, self-imposed sanctions may be subject to greater scrutiny and enforcement, but most importantly, the study and practice of CSR is likely to introduce new managerial institutions that can coexist with growing public, social, and environmental expectations of corporate conduct. Social change advocacy is already responding to the governance responsibility convergence by engaging in a vigorous debate over the future of CSR, as described earlier. One can expect that the conceptual disagreement between change agents who favour CSR and those who are critical of it, will not prevent the movement from strengthening and deepening its interface with corporate governance. In fact, the growing voice that seeks a "third way" between endorsing CSR and rejecting it is likely to gain support not only in the academia but also among practitioners and activists.

Similar to the potential outcomes in business regulation, social change advocacy will likely adapt to changes that are both formative and substantive in nature. Formative changes will potentially present new tactics for socially sensitive investors, NGOs, and public-interest organisations to work more closely with businesses to try and modify corporate practices through dialogue and negotiations. Changing tactics may also yield the devotion of more resources to consulting and providing guidance and expertise, at the expense of more traditional legislative or administrative advocacy.

The latter category of potential changes may lead the social justice movement to embark on new journeys, such as proposing concrete steps for business law and policy reform. For example, public groups in the CSR field may recommend new guidelines for companies on how to disclose social information and how to compensate their shareholders and executives while increasing other stakeholders' share of the pie. Such proposals for corporate reform from the public and non-profit sectors could maintain the long-term goals of social welfare while accommodating business needs that are inherent to the creation of economic wealth in market economies.

8.3   The Development Agencies and CSR

Initially, CSR was a corporate initiative adopted by individual companies and their organisations. In the late 1990s, it began to be taken up by international organisations such as the World Bank and the United Nations, and national development cooperation agencies such as Department for International Development (DFID) in the UK and the Canadian International Development Agency (CIDA).

The emergence of CSR as a development issue has to be seen in the context of the changing views of the development agencies on the main objectives of development and the best means of bringing it about. Over the past quarter century, the view of development as being primarily about economic growth has become less dominant, with a much greater emphasis on the social dimensions of development as exemplified by the creation of the Human Development Index by the United Nations Development Programme. This shift culminated in the adoption of the UN Millennium Development Goals (MDGs), focused on eradicating poverty and hunger, achieving universal primary education, promoting gender equality, reducing mortality and improving health, and ensuring environmental sustainability, among others. Poverty was a key target for the MDGs, which aimed to reduce the proportion of the world's population living on less than US$1 a day by half between 1990 and 2015.

A second feature of the changing view of the development agencies in this period was the decline in confidence in the role of the state as an agent for development. That was most vividly illustrated in the emergence, in the 1980s, of the 'Washington Consensus', which emphasised on liberalisation, deregulation and a reduced role for the state in developing economies – and a correspondingly greater role for the private sector. This shift of emphasis was also reflected in the flows of capital to developing countries, where FDI was running at three times the level of official development assistance (ODA). You need reference here when you compare volumes of ODA with FDI.

Market failures may prevent business operating in a socially responsible fashion. If firms are driven by short-term financial profitability, they may not make the long-term investments necessary to promote human development or benefit the poor. For example, training which would help develop employees' capabilities might not be provided because the returns are not immediate.

There are grounds, therefore, for thinking that firms which are concerned only or primarily with the financial bottom line would not meet these social objectives. On the other hand, socially responsible business could be expected to seek to overcome these obstacles in order to ensure a wider spread of benefits. It is against this background that the development agencies have come to see CSR as a way of reconciling support for private enterprise and a market-based system with their central aim of reducing global poverty.

A pioneer in promoting CSR in a development context was DFID, which created a Socially Responsible Business Unit in 1997, following the publication of the first White Paper on International Development which committed the Department to promoting ethical business and voluntary codes of conduct on core labour standards. The unit was involved in establishing the Ethical Trading Initiative in 1998 and creating a Resource

Centre for the Social Dimensions of Business Practice in 1999. The second White Paper also saw an important role for CSR in poverty reduction, devoting a section of the chapter on 'Harnessing Private Finance' to the issue. The multilateral development agencies have also been active in promoting CSR in recent years. The World Bank took up the CSR banner in the late 1990s. CSR Practice was set up within the Private Sector Development. It was located within the Private Sector Advisory Service Department, advising developing countries governments on ways to deploy and encourage CSR. The training arm of the Bank, the World Bank Institute, organises periodic electronic conferences on CSR and has been involved in offering training courses in this area (World Bank, 2003; 2006).

The Inter-American Development Bank has also engaged in the promotion of corporate responsibility, holding an annual conference on the subject. In 2000, the UN launched the Global Compact, which involves business, labour, NGOs and governments. Its original nine principles were derived from the Universal Declaration of Human Rights, the International Labour Organisation's (ILO) Fundamental Principles on Rights at Work and the Rio Declaration on Environment and Development (Cordero, Zúñiga and M. Rueda, 2014; ILO, 2012).

Critics have pointed to a tendency for the Global Compact Office, as an example of an international bank operating in East Africa that wanted to provide banking services tailored to poor customers who did not have access to affordable credit, current accounts and savings services. The project was vetoed by the head office in London on the grounds that it was risky and did not meet the 30% rate of return required by the bank on such risky investments on the promotion of FDI in developing countries as an important objective and even to regard it as a manifestation of corporate responsibility (Nyuur, Ofori and Debrah, 2015; OECD, 2000).

8.3.1 Foreign Direct Investment and Poverty

The challenge of reducing poverty and improving living conditions of the poor is formidable. Reducing poverty requires a growing economy with an increasing number of people working in higher value-added industries. Although poverty reduction has not been an explicit element of CSR, it does not necessarily mean that the adoption of socially responsible business practices has no impact on poverty in developing countries. In order to address this question more directly, it is necessary first to consider the ways in which business and particularly FDI can contribute to poverty reduction. Given the increased significance of FDI as a source of capital for developing countries in recent years, and the emphasis of development agencies on poverty reduction as a prominent goal, it is surprising that research on the impact of FDI on poverty is so limited.

The paucity of research on FDI and poverty in part reflects the fact that many consider the major potential contribution of FDI to poverty reduction to be through its impact on growth. While some authors like Ofori-Brobbey, Ojode, and Woldie (2010) and Ruskie (2007) find a positive relationship, many others point to the fact that this depends critically on local capabilities to absorb FDI and on the local policy framework, suggesting the need for caution in drawing any direct causal relationship. Therefore, if FDI does lead to higher growth, and provided that this is not offset by increased income inequality, then increased FDI will lift some people out of poverty. However, this tells us very little about the actual mechanisms linking FDI to poverty reduction.

8.3.2 *Corporate Social Responsibility and Poverty Reduction*

Most of the resource allocations in any market economies are undertaken by the markets. While re-distributions are often implemented by the central authorities, many people are left out from the comfort zones and are therefore trapped in poverty. Several attempts to rescue the poor by formal market and policy arrangement often do not achieve significant results, leading to several still wallowing in poverty. Dusuki and Dar (2005) show that several driving forces like growing market pressure on social and ethical issues, regulatory pressure, and increased power of communication may worsen poverty, thereby propelling emergence of CSR as solution.

The gap created has been filled in the past by the actions of many corporations which felt that giving back to the society will reduce poverty and make the environment they operate more conducive to business. In rendering the CSR as a poverty alleviating measures, most companies tend to focus on the upper and middle class, but there is a huge potential of consumers who have little disposable income but are a promising market if businesses can rethink their strategies (Kamrujjaman and Nisa, 2016). These authors further posited that whenever organisations, companies and businesses contribute to the community, they are giving back to the people.

The objective of the business enterprise is to maximise profit, though the long run survival of the business often hinges on the relationship the business has with the society. This relationship is often achieved through CSR activities, which endear the business to the people. It creates mutual benefits for the business and the people, many of whom have their economic status elevated. CSR can reduce poverty among the people in many different ways.

CSR is not only achieved through philanthropic strides but also by managing the business such that it benefits as many stakeholders as possible. When business is managed in such a way that it creates employment for many individuals in its community, unemployment declines, income of the community rises through wage earnings and market spill overs and poverty level reduces. This channel through which CSR reduces poverty is called the enterprise channel (Pradhan, 2007). By trading its product in the community, economic activities of the community improve, and poverty reduces through this distribution channel. Also, by generating revenue and paying taxes to the governments, companies contribute to poverty reduction. As governments use tax revenue to build infrastructure and improves economic well-being of the people, CSR in form of tax payment to the government, help reduce poverty through the government revenue channel (Pradhan, 2007).

8.4   CSR: The NDIC Experience

In the last 29 years, the Corporation has been actively involved in voluntary actions executed outside its statutory mandate, which are basically intended to positively impact on its various stakeholders. Apart from being a public institution, which should ordinarily participate in courses of action that serve the public interest, the Corporation has passionately pursued other developmental activities as part of its corporate social responsibility.

Towards promoting educational excellence and in the fulfilment of its social responsibility, the Corporation instituted, in 1994, an endowment fund and prize awards for institutions of higher learning in the country. Under the scheme, grants were made to several universities. A total of nine universities benefitted from the endowment of Professorial Chairs in different academic fields by 1995. Similarly, in 1996, thirty-one universities benefitted from cash award prizes with some getting two prize awards.

The Board of the Corporation subsequently decided in 2003 to sponsor projects in institutions of higher learning instead of the hitherto endowment/prize awards. That represented a response to the challenge thrown by the federal government in 2003, to Bankers' Committee on the deplorable state of infrastructural facilities in the higher institutions of learning in the country. Thus, in 2003, the Board of the Corporation approved a grant of ₦130 million to be disbursed at the rate of ₦10 million each to thirteen selected federal universities. Two universities each from the six geo-political zones of the country and one from the FCT were selected for the grant. The projects, which were conceived and executed by the institutions, included lecture halls, academic offices, students' hostels, lecture theatres, provision of laboratory equipment, internet facilities and cybercafé/computer centres that were considered essential for effective learning and research. By 2006, the implementation of the various projects under the above grant was virtually completed. In the same year, the Board of the Corporation approved another disbursement of funds under the initiative thereby bringing the cumulative amount disbursed under the first and second phases of the project-based support to ₦250 million with beneficiaries rising to twenty-five universities and polytechnics spread across the six geo-political zones.

In view of the rising cost of materials and to ensure the successful completion of the projects, the maximum grant extended by the Corporation to educational institutions was reviewed upwards in 2011 from ₦10 million to ₦20 million per project under the third phase of the initiative. In the third phase, eleven institutions were beneficiaries of ₦20 million each. The assistance, through the project-based support funding scheme, had contributed significantly towards the enhancement of learning environment and had promoted excellence in educational activities to move the country forward on the path of social and economic development.

Beyond the support to educational institutions, the Corporation took responsibility for the publication of the *Nigerian Banking Law Reports*. The publication is a compendium of decided banking-related cases in Nigeria. It documented all banking and finance cases decided by the courts since 1933. That was part of its contribution to the development of the legal profession in Nigeria.

In a recent survey conducted by an independent consultant on the status of the various education projects that were executed, the Corporation noted with satisfaction that all the projects were serving the purposes for which they were executed. Beneficiaries were full of commendation for the efforts and wished other corporate bodies should emulate the NDIC.

8.5 Conclusion

Corporate social responsibility plays a vital role in reducing poverty and improving living condition when a particular country put in place proper mechanism that would ensure an organisation behaves in a manner that would facilitate the achievement of its economic objective without compromising social and environmental values of a society. However, the contribution of MNCs in Africa is minimal compared to what is obtainable in developed economies.

References

Carroll, A.B. (1999). Corporate Social Responsibility: Evolution of a Definitional Construct. *Business and Society*, 38 (3), 268-295

Cordero, J., Zúñiga, T. O. and M. Rueda (2014). Disability and corporate social responsibility reporting.

Dusuki, A. and H. Dar (2005). 'Stakeholders Perception of Corporate Social Responsibility of Islamic Banks: Evidence from Malaysia Economy'

Elkington, J. (1998). Partnerships from cannibals with forks: The triple bottom line of 21st century business. *Environmental Quality Management*, 8(1), 37-51

Frederick W., Post J., Davis K. E. (1992). *Business and Society: Corporate Strategy, Public Policy, Ethics*, 7th edn. McGraw-Hill: London

Freeman E. and Reed D. (1983). Stockholders and Stakeholders: A New Perspective on Corporate Governance. *California Management Review* 25(3),88-106

International Labour Organization (2012). 'International Instruments and Corporate Social Responsibility'

Ivanov A. and Peleah M. (2008). 'From centrally planned development to human development' UNDP Human Development Research Paper 2010/38

Kamrujjaman and Nisa, (2016). 'Poverty eradication through the corporate social responsibility (CSR) initiatives: A case study on two selected banks in Bangladesh', *International Journal of Applied Research*, Vol. 2, no. 9, pp. 43-50

Kent Greenfield, Saving the World with Corporate Law? 12-16, 23-31, (Boston College Law School, Research Paper No. 130, 2007)

Michael C. Jensen, Value Maximization, Stakeholder Theory, and the Corporate Objective Function, 14 J. APPLIED CORP. FIN. 8, 10-13, 16-20 (2001)

Nyuur, R. B., Ofori, D. F. and Y. A. Debrah (2015). 'The Impact of FDI Inflow on Domestic Firms' Uptake of CSR Activities: The Moderating Effects of Host Institutions', *Thunderbird International Business Review*, Vol. 58, issue 2, pp.147-159

Ofori-Brobbey, K., Ojode, L., & Woldie, M. (2010). Achieving goal congruence between the objectives of multinational enterprises (MNEs) and developing countries (DCs). *Journal of International Management Studies*, 5(1), 138-146

Paul H. *et al* (1999), New York: *Natural Capitalism: Creating the Next Industrial Revolution* 1-21, 144-169

Pradhan, J. (2007). 'Corporate Social Responsibility and Poverty CSR' ORG Centre for Social Research

Prahalad C.K., (2004). *The Fortune at the Bottom of the Pyramid*, University of Pennsylvania, Published by Wharton School, India.

Ruskie, T. G. (2007). Trends and determinants of inward foreign direct investment to South Africa

OECD (2000). 'Foreign Direct Investment, Development and Corporate Responsibility.

United Nations Development Programme, Human Development Reports, various Years, New York: Oxford University Press. Globalisation with a Human Face (1999) and Economic Growth and Human Development.

World Bank (2003). 'Strengthening implementation of corporate social responsibility in global supply chains.

World Bank (2006). Beyond Corporate Social Responsibility: The Scope for Corporate Investment in Community-Driven Development.

9

OFFICIAL SAFETY-NETS AND STAKEHOLDERS' PROTECTION DURING BANKING CRISIS: THE ROLE OF DEPOSIT INSURANCE[9]

9.0 Introduction

A financial safety-net is a framework that includes the prudential regulation, supervision, resolution, lender/guarantor of last resort and deposit insurance, all aimed at promoting sustainable confidence in the financial sector. Practically, therefore, safety-net refers to measures undertaken by relevant government agencies to help financial institutions in periods of crisis to shore up the confidence of various stakeholders, both as borrowers and creditors. In many jurisdictions, various departments of government such as Ministry of Finance/Treasury, Central Banks and Deposit Insurance Institutions are generally responsible for the technical

---

9   Original version of this paper was presented at a Workshop on Managing Banking Sector Crisis organised by the CBN held at CBN Minna Branch from 26th-28th April, 2010.

and financial support (IADI, 2018). These institutions provide support when a financial institution is hit by financial crisis in order to maintain safety and stability in the financial sector and the economy at large.

The rest of the chapter is divided into seven sections, Section 9.1 reviews the role of Deposit Insurance within the Nigeria safety-net; Section 9.2 discusses the expansion of government-provided guarantees in response to crises; Section 9.3 analyses the role of Deposit Insurance during crisis; Section 9.4 looks at the challenges; Section 9.5 reviews the critical success factors; while Section 9.6 discusses the NDIC experience as a safety-net participants and Section 9.7 concludes the chapter.

9.1 Deposit Insurance within the Nigeria Safety-Net

The roles and responsibilities assigned to safety-net operators in Nigeria are in line with international best practice, with the Federal Ministry of Finance as the guarantor of the lender of last resort and the Central Bank of Nigeria (CBN) as lender of last resort. Supervision is handled jointly by the CBN and the NDIC, while Deposit Insurance is handled solely by the NDIC.

As already stated elsewhere, it is worth refreshing our memory that the problem of bank failures in Nigeria began in the 1950s and climaxed in the late 1980s, when twenty-five out of twenty-eight banks collapsed without any form of protection to the affected depositors. Looking at the negative impact of bank failures on the general economic activities, the IMF, in 1986 under the SAP, recommended to the federal government the need to establish an explicit deposit protection scheme in Nigeria (NDIC, 2009).

Apart from the deposit insurance scheme implemented for the licensed banks, other customers who patronise ancillary financial services do not enjoy such protection and are therefore completely exposed in the event of insolvency and failure of any institution operating in those sub-sectors.

As a deposit protection agency, the concern of the NDIC is whether banks can prudently diversify into securities and insurance businesses without jeopardising depositors' funds. For instance, banks could utilise depositors' funds to make bad loans, either to assist securities affiliates or to protect the securities underwritten by such affiliates. It is also possible that depositors fund could be utilised by banks to purchase equity securities or for proprietary trading in stocks. The deposit insurance was established to strengthen the financial system to withstand bank runs; ensure financial system stability and integrity; promote competitive efficiency of the system, protect the depositors and the banking public and ensure orderly failure resolution of failing and failed financial institutions (Ibrahim, 2017).

The different components of the safety-net interact frequently to facilitate the attainment of its objectives. Though their primary mandates differ, each member of the safety-net faces a similar trade-off between avoiding disruptions and reducing moral hazards. Depending on the arrangements in a country, the providers of the safety-net facilities usually collaborate because of the interdependent nature of the components of the financial system. Traditionally, safety-net elements such as deposit insurance and lender-of-the-last-resort functions have evolved with focus on deposit-taking institutions to mitigate the risk of financial uncertainty, especially during financial crisis (Ogunleye, 2010).

9.2 Expansion of Government-Provided Guarantees in Response to Crises

9.2.1 *The Nigerian Experience*

Two major initiatives are emphasised in this section. These are:

i. Regulatory Intervention in 8 banks (Aug/Oct 2009).

ii. Expansion of Deposit Insurance Coverage.

In 2009, the CBN listed a number of factors that caused the banking crises of that period. These include macroeconomic instability, weak corporate governance in banks, poor risk management practices, inadequate disclosure regime, and weak supervision/enforcement. To tackle the crises, as pointed out earlier, top executive management of eight banks were removed from office, while stress test was conducted on ten banks which necessitated the injection of ₦620 billion as tier 2 capital into ailing banks adjudged to be in grave state with deficiencies in capital adequacy (Sanusi, 2011).

There was also the provision of deposit guarantee for all depositors, and the Federal Government declaration that no bank will be allowed to fail. Expectedly, cost was a major determinant in the choice of resolution options. The cost of resolution, particularly when it involves direct injection of fund by government or government guarantee, has three elements: direct fiscal allocation which would crowd out funds for other uses; contingent fiscal obligation in the case of guarantee; and moral hazard issues it generates (Ogunleye, 2010).

9.3 Role of Deposit Insurance during Crisis

A Deposit Insurance Scheme (DIS) is a financial guarantee to depositors, in the event of a bank failure. As a deposit protection scheme, it is usually supported by insured institutions themselves and administered either through a government-controlled agency; a privately held one or one that is jointly owned and administered. The broad roles of the deposit insurer are prevention of disruption to the payment system, maintaining and reinforcing public confidence, supporting solvent banks, and provision of expertise for resolution and liquidation of failed banks. What specific action is taken depends on the situation at hand, but the range of options may include:

i.   Increasing the deposit coverage level;
ii. Reducing the role of co-insurance arrangements;
iii. Taking steps to ensure timely access to insured deposits;
iv. Increasing the number of guaranteed institutions;
v.   Expanding the range of deposit products covered; and
vi. Implementing systemic stabilisation measure.

The deposit insurer may adjust the coverage upwards for a limited period of time as was done in the USA and many European countries during the crisis of 2007-2009, or the DIS agency may introduce unlimited retail deposit coverage as was done in some other countries in the same period. In the case of the latter, announcements to that effect could either be made explicitly or implicitly in statements by policymakers that all retail deposits are covered by a government guarantee (Ogunleye, 2010).

During each period, it is necessary to reduce the role of co-insurance (being an arrangement whereby depositors are protected up to a certain limit, beyond which depositors are required to bear part of the cost in case of banking failure). The usual practice was for the deposit insurer to drastically reduce such co-insurance or abolish same entirely. The latter was the case in many European countries during the recent global financial crisis (Umar, 2013).

Also, steps need to be taken to ensure timely access to insured deposits. This is important as the level of the coverage and as confidence-enhancing measure during the period of crisis. It is vital for the bank regulator/deposit insurer to embark on failure resolution mechanisms that can support effectiveness of deposit insurance and reduce the time of accessing insured deposits. Additionally, the deposit insurer could extend coverage to a wider range of deposits beyond those that are usually covered during normal times, extend guarantee temporarily to other deposit products and perhaps to other forms of unsecured debts. In jurisdictions where there are no explicit deposit insurance, crisis situation offers an opportunity to put one in place.

Coverage should be offered to a wider range of institutions including non-bank financial institutions; such as insurance companies, cooperative societies and large mutual funds. Extending coverage to these types of institutions would limit the spill-over effect on other financial institutions as well as the overall economy. Deposit insurers could act as receivers and liquidators of non-bank financial institutions which are presently subjected to normal insolvency resolution under the Companies Act. Such measures could minimise costs and possible reputational risks to policy makers arising from the potential social issues as the fall-out of the financial crisis (NDIC, 2013).

9.4 Challenges

The deposit insurer is confronted with a number of challenges, including a rise in moral hazards, if coverage is increased and especially if the limit is not capped. Thus, there is the need to put in place measures to check risky behaviours of players in the banking system. Such measures should include market discipline and specifying defined period when the enhanced deposit insurance coverage limit and blanket guarantees imposed by monetary authorities during period of banking crisis will end. The timeline should be guided by credible data.

Also, funding issues can constitute a challenge because the roles of deposit insurer are expanded during a crisis situation. Adequate funding is always a critical issue and it is important to maintain an appropriate ratio between the size of deposit insurance fund and the amount of total insured deposits. Funding levels can turn out to be inadequate in the face of unprecedented and systemic bank failures. Hence, it is important to specify the manner in which funds would be raised beyond what is available through accumulation of premiums. However, the NDIC Act provides in Section 36(1) & (2) that during periods of funding shortfalls, the NDIC can borrow from the CBN and/or receive CBN guarantee on any debenture stocks raised by the Corporation.

Another challenge relates to issues that may arise due to the co-existence of different levels of depositor protection, resulting from the fact that the provision of guarantees might provide some financial institutions or sectors with unfair competitive advantages, leading to shifts of deposits across institutions. The unfair advantage could be vis-a-vis other forms of savings (e.g. close substitutes to bank deposits) or vis-a-vis other deposit-taking institutions that do not enjoy the guarantee. One approach to resolving the challenge is to widen the guarantee to other forms of deposits or bank liabilities and institutions, but the difficult issue arises as to where to draw the line.

The possibility of massive shifts of deposits as a result of differences in the generosity of deposit insurance systems across countries is also something to watch. Within a country, different levels of deposit insurance for host country banks and branches of foreign banks can give rise to consumer protection issues. All the challenges must be factored in when a deposit insurer is deciding on what to do during a crisis (Umar, 2013).

9.5 Critical Success Factors

The critical success factors necessary for effective and efficient execution of the role of DIS in a crisis situation include:

- having a clearly defined mandate and powers;
- sound governance/operational independence; and
- access to funding.

It is also necessary for the deposit insurer to be flexible in dealing with crisis, be equipped with a comprehensive tool box, and have the discretion to employ these tools to intervene early, to find the least cost resolution options that are less disruptive to the financial system and public confidence. Close cooperation with other safety-net players, and effective public awareness are important considerations (Birchi, 2014).

9.6 NDIC Experience

NDIC is a risk minimiser with the mandates to insure deposits, monitor the financial health condition of the insured institutions and provide orderly mechanism for failure resolution.

For the effective delivery of its mandate, the Corporation has the following sources of funding:

i.   Capital contribution by government;
ii. Premium collection from insured institutions, the aggregation of which translates to its Insurance Funds (DIF);
iii. Premium surcharge on insured institutions; and
iv. Borrowing from the CBN, the Federal Ministry of Finance.

The provision in the Fiscal Responsibility Act of 2007 which requires the Corporation to pay 80% of its operating surplus into the Federal Government Revenue Account, has impaired the growth of the insurance fund.

In 2009, the NDIC participated in the special examination of twenty-four banks with the CBN, which revealed that 10 banks were in grave financial condition.

Specific responses of the NDIC to the findings were the proposal to amend the NDIC Act (2006) in order to strengthen the Corporation in enforcing and reimbursing depositors' funds promptly. The Corporation reviewed the deposit insurance coverage upwards from ₦200,000 and ₦100,000 for Deposit Money Banks and Microfinance Banks/Primary Mortgage Banks respectively to ₦500,000 and ₦200,000 maximum deposit. Coverage limit for Primary Mortgage Banks was later raised from ₦200,000 to ₦500,000 in 2016. The Corporation has enhanced its public awareness campaigns, and capacity building efforts through recruitment of new staff as well as upgrading the skills of existing staff in focused areas of Risk-Based Supervision (RBS), Enterprise Risk Management (ERM), Consolidated Supervision and Failure Resolution. The Corporation also conducted target examination of MFBs in collaboration with the CBN, to determine their physical existence as well as their financial condition. It had also enhanced its debt recovery mechanism by appointing professional debt recovery agents. In view of the importance of Information Technology (IT) to the success of any modern enterprise, there were deliberate effort by the Corporation to strengthen its IT infrastructure. Finally, collaboration with other members of the Financial Services Regulation Coordinating Committee (FSRCC) in the areas of macro-prudential regulation and supervision was rigorously pursued (Habu, 2013).

9.7 Conclusion

The global financial crisis of 2007-2008 has reshaped the structure of financial safety-net worldwide with government playing the role of guarantor-of-lender-of-last-resort providing deposit guarantees especially during the period of intense bank failures help to raise the confidence of depositors, thereby stalling the occurence of any bank run in period of banking crisis. Recent changes to deposit insurance parameters in many countries, following the global financial crisis, are indeed just one type of a variety of comprehensive measures undertaken to restore confidence and support financial intermediation. They do not substitute for other measures that directly address the root causes of the lack of confidence; rather, they increase the need for these measures as quick responses and shoring up confidence before the measures that tackle the root causes of the crisis take effect.

The need to ensure the confidence of depositors, especially the small unsophisticated savers, is crucial since they are essentially the conduit to entrance supply of stable funds for intermediation by banks, even during financial crisis periods.

References

Birchi H. (2014). "Public Awareness and Deposit Insurance in Nigeria" Paper presented at the NDIC Academy

Habu, K. (2013). "NDIC as a Financial Safety-net" *Business Day* publication 20th May

IADI (2018). "Financial Safety-Net", www.iadi.org, Definitions of terms in the organisation's website

Ibrahim, U. (2017). IADI Core Principles for effective Deposit Insurance Scheme Being a paper presented at the Conference on Resolution and Deposit Insurance, Cape Town, South Africa

NDIC (2009-2013). Annual Reports

Ogunleye G.A. (2010). "Perceptions on the Nigeria Financial Safety Net" *NDIC* publication.

Sanusi, L. S. (2011). 'Global financial meltdown and the reforms in the Nigerian banking sector', *CBN Journal of Applied Statistics*. Vol. 2 No.1, pp. 93-108

Umar, M. Y. (2013). "Financial Safety-net and Deposit Insurance." Paper presented at the NDIC Academy

10

FINANCIAL SYSTEM RESILIENCE IN A GLOBALISED ECONOMY: PROSPECTS, THREATS AND BENEFITS TO THE NIGERIAN FINANCIAL SECTOR

10.0 Introduction

Although, there is no universal consensus regarding its definition, globalisation can be viewed from both the broad and narrow perspectives. In broad terms, globalisation is seen as the expansion of global linkages, the organisation of social life on a global scale and the growth of a global consciousness and consolidation of world society across various dimensions like economic, political, security, environmental, health, social and cultural lines. From a narrow perspective, however, it refers to economic integration, through which economies of various societies are weaved together by way of trade, finance and investment, as well as migration and flows of information and technology. The focus of this chapter is on the narrow definition of globalisation.

Though the integration in terms of trade flows has been huge, the rate of financial globalisation has been more pronounced, especially in the last few decades. This has been marked by unprecedented flows of financial assets and liabilities (foreign direct investment, portfolio flows, debt and other flows) across borders, and removal of policy restraints on such flows by many countries (Smulker, 2003). As it stands, no modern economy can be considered closed in the traditional sense, as most facets of socio-economic life in different countries have intermixed because national geographical borders no longer serve as barriers to the integration of human activities in a highly globalised world. Nations and countries separated by formidable geographical distances are now closer than ever imagined with the dynamic advancement in information and communication technology. The cross-inflow of economic activities, especially in trade and finance since centuries past (Srinivasan, 2013), in scale, structure and speed, in no way matches the current monumental levels that globalisation (whether financial or economic) has fostered across industries and countries' borders. This explains why most studies on globalisation are focussed on financial liberalisation. Besides, because the effects of financial flows on real sector growth are significant and complex, underscores why it attracts much interest in the literature (Obstfeld and Taylor, 2003; Caprio et al, 2006).

Financial globalisation has been embraced by many developing economies following observed benefits enjoyed by financially integrated developed nations. These benefits include, among others, provision of liquidity and capital to bridge saving-investment gaps; improvement of the financial system infrastructure and efficiency through reduction in asymmetric information problem; and risk sharing and diversification. The promotion of global corporate governance best practices and decrease in likelihood of bail outs, as foreign banks participate in local financial sector; spill over in financial technology and financial products that deepen the financial markets; increased utility to financial market participants; promotion of growth and development of participating economies, are some of the added advantages of integration.

Many of these benefits have, however, been elusive to many developing economies as local realities in these countries are not strongly supportive of globalisation gains. In this light, many studies have argued that financial globalisation has had little or no growth effects in developing countries (Mishkin, 2007; Rodrik and Subramanian, 2009). Others, however, argued that benefit realisation is conditional on specific characteristics of the economy, including the depth of its financial sector (Klein and Olivei, 2008), initial financial conditions and the quality of its policies and institutions.

In many occasions, financial integration has imposed macroeconomic challenges on financially open economies by inducing financial system fragility and macroeconomic volatility. Several economies experience currency appreciation during booms of capital inflows and consequently lost their trade competitiveness. Excessive credit growth that trails financial sector liquidity, reduces credit quality and heightens the potential for non-performing loans. Sudden reversals of capital inflows, following global credit crunch, reduce capital availability for investment and thus have adverse growth effects. Generally, there have been increasing empirical evidence that financial globalisation increases financial and macroeconomic risks including, but not limited to macroeconomic instability and vulnerability to financial crises (Stavarek *et al*, 2012; Abraham and Smulker, 2017).

Vital to curtailing these challenges is the concept of financial system resilience which has been identified by Gregorio (2013), as an important factor that stimulated economic recovery of Latin America from the financial crisis of 2008. Without this resilience, the effects of other recovery determinants such as supportive terms of trade, exchange rate flexibility and fiscal and monetary expansion may not have been able to sustain the growth of the economy in crisis. The resilience is however not unconnected with prior reforms and regulation of the financial sector as was the case of Nigeria whose earlier financial sector reforms and the build-up of reserves enabled the economy to wade through the 2008 financial crisis, compared to many other economies, especially on the African continent. Details of these reforms and how they had prepared the financial sector for resilience against the crises are subsequently discussed.

Section 10.1 discusses the 2007 global financial crises, its propagation and how the Nigerian financial system sector was affected by the contagion. Section 10.2 highlights factors affecting the resilience of the Nigerian banking system and policy implementation to strengthen it. The role of deposit insurance in Nigeria and the activities of the NDIC in entrenching financial sector resilience are presented in Section 10.3. Section 10.4 presents concluding remarks.

10.1 Global Financial Crises Contagion and the Nigerian Financial System

Global financial crisis is an international phenomenon that affects many economies negatively within the same period. Summers (2008) conceptualised international financial crisis as national financial crisis exacerbated by international factors. Thus, the financial crisis that swept across many nations in the 1990s at different periods had international dimension because external and international factors played significant roles in them. Examples of such international financial crises were the Asian financial crisis affecting Thailand, Indonesia, South Korea and the Latin American crises that besieged Brazil and Mexico (Kaminsky and Reinhart, 1998). However, there are many other financial crises that may not be deemed as international as they were largely induced by domestic factors. Such included the 'Big Five' crises that occurred in Spain in 1977, Norway in 1987; Finland in 1991; Sweden in 1991; and Japan in 1992 (Reinhart and Rogoff, 2008). Other non-international financial crises many of which were fuelled by domestic bank crisis, included financial crises in Australia in 1989; Canada in 1983, Germany in 1977; Greece in 1991; and Italy in 1990.

While domestic factors may not be downplayed, the crises either began or worsened by the influence of international macroeconomic factors. For instance, while corporate governance and moral hazard played a role in the Asian financial crisis, availability of international capital market liquidity, signalled by low interest rates in industrialised countries, especially Japan, was a key factor (Corsetti *et al*, 1999). The impact of the crises resulted in a painful economic recession in these countries and the ravaging sub-optimal economic outcome. The crises were almost invariably preceded by a period of prolonged boom in economic activities, fuelled by credit creation and surges in capital flows. In other words, financial globalisation, and the associated flows of capital following financial liberalisation are at the root of financial crisis.

At the centre of global financial crises is the financial system that acts as the conduit for international capital flow. While the flows of these capital are usually the result of policy-induced economic imbalance between countries, the effects on the lending and credit management behaviour of the international financial intermediaries contribute significantly to prolonging the crisis.

Like in other countries before the 2007 global financial crises, the Nigerian financial sector experienced cross-border flows of capital of significant magnitude. The inflow of international capital (whether foreign direct investment and portfolio equity) were so large, that the Nigerian Stock Exchange All-Share Index (ASI) rose by 74.7% in 2007, culminating in equity market capitalisation hitting ₦12.6 trillion in first quarter of 2008 (Sanusi, 2011). The inflows to the country however significantly fell in the wake of the crisis, and that triggered stock market slumps (Sanusi, 2011). Margin loans default rose as banks recalled credit to stock market financing and the stock market performance drastically fell as ASI and market capitalisation declined by 33.8% and 28.5%, respectively, in 2009.

The global financial crisis hit the Nigerian economy through financial integration and contagion. The financial linkage and interconnectedness of local banks and foreign international banks provided the medium for propagation of shocks from foreign, especially developed economies to Nigeria. The crises-induced decline in global demand negatively affected oil price and further reduced the government fiscal space and capacity to exploit fiscal policy alternatives to revamp the economy. That worsened the economic situation and the effectiveness of monetary policy was limited by the weak position of the banks following the crisis. The country was however, fortunate to have reformed her financial sector before the crisis. The sector was therefore in the position to successfully weather through the crisis. The effects of crisis on the economy was therefore minimal.

10.2 Building Financial Sector Resilience in Nigeria: A Necessity for Economic Growth and Stability

The Nigerian economy was in tumultuous state prior to the global financial crisis. The unstable banking environment had lingered before independence, and that was due to lax policy and regulatory arrangement. Before the Central Bank of Nigeria (CBN) was established in 1958, there was hardly any discrete financial regulatory agency with firm bank supervisory roles. Many commercial banks in the pre-CBN era, operated without the guidance of a firm regulatory framework. Most of the banks established in that colonial era failed: twenty-one out of twenty-five indigenous banks collapsed by 1954 due to absence of regulatory standard prior Banking Ordinance of 1952 (Ogunleye, 2002). The failures stemmed from various perennial structural problems militating against the establishment and performance of indigenous banks in Nigeria such as mismanagement, managerial incompetence, fraud and embezzlement (Newlyn and Rowan, 1954) and non-cooperative attitude and denigration by the colonial banks.

Following the establishment of the CBN in 1958, commercial banks behaviour became more ethical, as they began to operate within specified standards. That led to stability (Egbo, 2012), less failure and lower requirements for resolutions by the CBN. The stability of the banking industry continued into 1970s, buoyed by the oil sector prosperity. The growth of the banking sector was however threatened in 1980s from the combined effects of poor management of available resources and unfavourable external environment occasioned by the collapse in crude oil prices. As a result, many banks were distressed before 1990.

To minimise risks of failure and effects on the system, the CBN Act 2007, as amended, the NDIC Act of 1988 and the Bank and Other Financial Institution Act, BOFIA 1991 as amended, were put in place. Banks were recapitalised, with the capital requirements for commercial raised from ₦20 million in 1989 to ₦50 million in 1990; and that of merchant banks increased from ₦12 million to ₦40 million over the same period. (Obienusi and Obienusi, 2015). Despite the reforms, banking sector conditions deteriorated (Sobodu and Akiode, 1994), and many banks still failed.

In response to the weak banking system, the banking recapitalisation reform was implemented in 2005 raising the capital base of all banks to ₦25 billion. The reform was aimed at correcting the deep structural problems, such as over-dependence on public sector funds and CBN credits as well as income from foreign exchange trading. Other problems of the banks were undercapitalisation, weak corporate governance, poor asset quality, inaccurate reporting, non-compliance with regulatory requirements, falling ethics and gross insider abuses, resulting in huge non-performing insider related credits. The oligopolistic structure in which 10 of the 89 banks then, controlled more than 50% of the industry assets and liabilities, lack of capacity to support the real sector of the economy, and lack of competition by banks in savings mobilisation to boost the level of deposits, constituted the other critical issues (Sanusi, 2011). Thirteen banks were unable to meet the requirement of the ₦25 billion by 31st December, 2005 and so, their licences were revoked in 2006 by the CBN and handed over to the NDIC for liquidation.

Despite these reforms, attempts by the Nigerian monetary and regulatory authorities to strengthen the resilience of Nigerian banking sector against both domestic and international financial crisis appeared insufficient. The sector proved weak to absorb financial shocks from the global crisis and to curtail their transmission into the economy. In 2009, the economy witnessed another banking crisis following the global financial crisis. Nine out of twenty-four banks were found to be insolvent, causing a serious risk to the Nigerian financial sector. Many other problems were prevalent, ranging from inadequacies in capital asset ratios and liquidity ratios, weaknesses in corporate governance and risk management practices, worrisome increase in non-performing loans (NPLs), as well as excessive exposure to the oil and gas sector.

Several policy initiatives were taken to further strengthen the Nigerian banking sector, increase its resilience against any form of shock, domestic or foreign, as means of engendering financial stability and promoting economic growth. While short-term measures like the independent audit of commercial banks, immediate replacement of top management of the affected banks were targeted at immediate resolution of problems at hand, especially that of restoring confidence to the banking public and financial investors (Sanusi, 2011), many others were for long-term repositioning of the sector. Following the audit findings, the CBN injected ₦620 billion in form of Tier 2 capital into ten marks found to be in grave state with deficiencies in capital adequacy into the nine banks in order to strengthen the banking industry, protect depositors and creditors, restore public confidence and safeguard the integrity of the Nigerian banking industry.

The long-term policy measures included the implementation of risk-based supervision, reforms to regulatory framework, enhancing reporting framework, as well as enhancing provisions for customer protection. Other measures were the establishment of macro-prudential policies, developing purposeful monetary and countercyclical fiscal policies and developing the capital market as an alternative source to bank funding. All these solutions were targeted at ensuring viability of the financial sector to support economic growth and development.

10.3 NDIC and Financial System Stability in Nigeria

The financial conditions of many banks were so precarious that Nigeria's financial system stability was threatened, as signalled by the large number of bank failures soon after they came into operation. In response to the challenge, the NDIC was established in 1988, and commenced operation in March 1989, to complement the efforts of the CBN in restoring confidence in Nigeria's financial system through the orderly resolution of bank distress and failures to guarantee safety of bank deposits in the event of collapse of the some banks in the system and minimise the knock-on effects of the financial crisis on the macro economy.

Both the NDIC and CBN had to exercise various failure resolution options based on the severity and peculiarity of bank distress. These ranged from provision of financial assistance, use of corrective action, assumption of control and management, restructuring, purchase and assumption, sale of distressed banks and liquidation of terminally distressed banks (Ogunleye, 2002). The regulatory and supervisory agencies extended financial assistance of ₦2.3 billion to 10 banks in 1989 to alleviate their liquidity challenges and restore public confidence in the banking sector (NDIC, 1989).

For banks whose failures could not be resolved through financial assistance, other resolution packages were applied (Kama, 2013). Also, Holding Actions were applied by both CBN and NDIC to several banks in 1994 and 1995, while many other banks were restructured and had their management replaced in 1993 and 2009. Furthermore, tougher resolution measures were used on banks with grave corporate financial conditions. These included 'acquisition' and 'take over' options (used in 1993, 1995 and 1996), Purchase and Assumption (used in 1993, 1996, 2006 and 2007), licence revocation, closure and liquidation.

In subsequent periods, the weak state of many banks was exposed, particularly in the wake of the global financial crisis. In response to this exposure, CBN/ NDIC conducted a special examination of twenty-four deposit money banks (DMBs) in 2009 and it was found that, ten of the banks were found to be unsound and were resolved through several resolution options (NDIC, 2011; Afolabi, 2011). The resolution mechanisms adopted included, licence revocation of one hundred and three MFBs in 2010, three DMBs in 2011, twenty-four PMBs in 2012 and one DMB in 2013; financial assistance through indirect liquidity injection by AMCON in the form of NPL purchase in 2011; use of bridge banks in 2011 to take over the three DMB closed in 2011; regulator-facilitated merger and acquisition (M&A) of five banks in 2011; sales of bridge banks by AMCON to investors in 2014 and 2017. The bridge banks were Mainstreet, Keystone and Enterprise Banks for former Afribank Plc, BankPHB Plc and Springbank Plc, respectively. The Bridge banks were immediately sold to AMCON through share subscription, while the banking licences of Afribank Plc, BankPHB Plc and Springbank Plc were revoked by the CBN. In 2018, the CBN revoked licence of Skye Bank and the NDIC established a bridge bank, Polaris Bank to assume the assets and liabilities of the defunct bank.

The activities of the NDIC, with the support of other members of Financial Services Regulation Coordinating Committee (FSRCC) – National Insurance Commission, Pension Commission and Security and Exchange Commission – have proved indispensable in resolving the crisis during the period. Accordingly, the Corporation contributed significantly towards improving the resilience and stability of the Nigerian financial system.

10.4   Conclusion

The financial sector serves as the medium of financial integration with the global world, and as the conduit for cross-border flows of international capital. It also doubles as the channel for allocating capital to the real sector. These roles make the financial sector important in economic growth process, and therefore attract attention from regulatory authorities. The Nigerian financial system has undergone several transformational challenges that threatened its very existence and ability to deliver on its role in economic growth and development process. In this light, several reforms to regulatory frameworks that guided the operation of the banking sector, as well as the capital market participant, were implemented.

The reforms were driven by members of the FRSCC. In collaboration with the CBN, Federal Ministry of Finance, SEC and other safety-net participants, the NDIC had undertaken several deposit insurance activities to revolutionise commercial banking operations, resolve inherent problems that could undermine their performance, as well as strengthen the contributions of the banking sector to economic growth.

Overall, the Nigerian economy has benefitted from the interaction with other economies through trade, investment and finance. While the real and financial integrations into the global economy context have been beneficial, they are not without their risks and costs. Foreign direct investment and portfolio equity and debt flows have assisted in bridging the saving-investment gaps and foreign exchange gap, but the sudden reversals of the flows during periods of financial crises had led to economic contraction, unemployment and severe welfare losses.

References

Abraham, F. and Schmukler, S. L. (2017). 'Financial globalisation: a glass half empty?' *World Bank Policy Research Working Paper* No. 8194

Afolabi, J. A. (2011). 'Merger and acquisition in the Nigeria banking system: issues and challenges', a paper presented at the workshop for business editors and finance correspondents association of Nigeria at Manpower Development Institute, Dutse, Jigawa State between November 28 – 29, 2011

Alley, I. S. (2015). 'Private Capital Flows and Economic Growth of Sub-Saharan African Countries', *African Development Review*, Vol. 27, Issue 4, pp. 469-483

Asongu, S. and De Moor, L. (2015). 'Financial globalisation dynamic thresholds for financial development: evidence from Africa', *European Journal of Development Research*, Vol. 29, Issue 1, pp. 192-212

Caprio, G., P. Honohan, and J. Stiglitz, (2006). *Financial Liberalization*. Cambridge, MA: Cambridge University Press.

Corsetti G., Paolo Pesentib, P. and Roubini, N. (1999). 'What caused the Asian currency and financial crisis?', *Japan and the World Economy*, Vol. 11, pp. 305-373

Egbo, O. P. (2012). 'Universal basis of bank failure – the Nigerian case', *Developing Country Studies*, Vol. 2, No. 10, pp. 119-131

Gregorio, J. (2013). "Resilience in Latin America; Lessons from macroeconomic management and Financial policies" IMF

Kama, U. (2013). Banking sector crisis and resolution options in Nigeria', *Central Bank of Nigeria Bullion,* Vol. 34, No. 1 pp. 7-18

Kaminsky, C. and Reinhart, G. (1998). 'Financial crises in Asia and Latin America: Then and now', *American Economic Review,* Vol. 88, No. 2, pp. 444-448.

Mishkin, F., (2007). 'Is Financial Globalisation Beneficial?', *Journal of Money, Credit and Banking,* Vol. 39, No 2-3, 259-294

NDIC (1989-2011). 'Annual Report and Statement of Accounts', A publication of the Nigeria Deposit Insurance Corporation

Newlyn, W. T. and D. C. Rowan (1954). *Money and Banking in British Colonial Africa,* Oxford, University Press

Obstfeld, M., and A. Taylor, (2003). 'Global Capital Markets: Integration, Crisis, and Growth', in M. Bordo, A. Taylor, and J. Williamson (eds.), *Globalisation in Historical Perspective.* Chicago, IL: University of Chicago Press

Obienusi, I. and E. A. Obienusi (2015). 'Banking reforms and the Nigeria economy, 1990-2007, *Historical Research Letter,* Vol. 21, pp. 17-42

Ogunleye, G. A. (2002). 'Deposit Insurance Scheme in Nigeria: Problems and Prospects', A paper presented at the first annual conference of

International Association of Deposit Insurers (IADI) in May, 2002

Reinhart C. M. and Rogoff K. S. (2008). 'Is the 2007 US Sub-Prime Financial Crisis So Different? An International Historical Comparison' *American Economic Review*, Vol. 98, No. 2, pp. 339-344

Rodrik, R. and A. Subramanian (2009). 'Why Did Financial Globalisation Disappoint?' *IMF Staff Papers*, Vol. 56, Issue (1), pp. 112-138

Sanusi, L. S. (2011). 'Global financial meltdown and the reforms in the Nigerian banking sector', *CBN Journal of Applied Statistics*, Vol. 2 No. 1, pp. 93-108

Schmukler, S. L. (2003). "Financial Globalisation: Gain and Pain for Developing countries. World Bank

Sobodu, O. O. and P. O. Akiode (1994). 'Bank performance, supervision and privatization in Nigeria: Analysing the transition to a deregulated economy', A paper presented at the Workshop of the African Economic Research Consortium, Nairobi, 3–8 December

Srinivasan, T. N. (2013). 'Trends and Impacts of Real and Financial Globalisation in the People's Republic of China and India since the 1980s' *Asian Development Review*, Vol. 30, No. 1, pp. 1–30

Stavarek, D., I. Repkova, and K. Gajdosova (2012). 'Theory of Financial Integration and Achievements in the European Union', in R. Matousek and

D. Stavarek (eds.), *Financial Integration in the European Union*. Abingdon: Routledge

11

BANK FAILURE RESOLUTION MEASURES:
NIGERIAN EXPERIENCE[10]

11.0 Introduction

The roles of the banking sector, financial safety-net, and other deposit taking financial institutions are important in the economy because of their involvement in the payments system, their roles as intermediaries between the surplus and deficit spending units of the economy as well as their functions as agents for transmission of monetary policy. The intermediary role of banks exposes them to risks of failure and loss of public confidence in their operations, if liquidity mismatch occurs that may become entrenched in the face of instability in socio-economic environment.

---

10   Original version of this paper was presented at the Regional Consultative Group Sub-Sahara Workshop on Recovery and Resolution Planning held in Ghana, May 6-9, 2014.

A deposit insurance is important to protect the banking system from instability, occasioned by dangers of bank runs and their contagion effects (Eisenbeis and Kaufmann, 2010). A key function of a deposit insurer is to institute an effective resolution regime to maintain financial system stability and confidence in the banking system. Depositor protection, through deposit insurance, is usually done either by an explicit DIS or an implicit arrangement (Kyei, 1995; Ibrahim, 2017).

Similarly, the importance of providing robust and effective "resolution regimes" that ensures safety of financial institutions (FIs), protects depositors' funds, limits moral hazards and minimises systemic disruption, is crucial to enhance financial system stability especially in developing economy, where there exist relatively large number of small unsophisticated despositors of particular importance in a developing economy. This is more so in Nigeria because of policy strategies to enhance financial inclusion and to reduce the number of the unbanked population. Over the years, the NDIC in its operations has put in place diverse failure resolution mechanisms and strategies aimed at resolving failed and failing financial institutions.

Effective resolution entails a series of systematic actions designed to end a bank's distressed condition with minimal disruption without exposing taxpayers to the burden of resuscitating failed banks (Afolabi, 2014). The objectives of Nigerian failure resolution regimes usually include depositor protection, minimising adverse effects on banking and financial system stability, ensuring continuity of basic banking functions, minimising reliance on public sector support, and protection of clients funds and assets (Anyadiegwu, 2017). In a bid to abide by best practices in resolution activities in most jurisdictions, regulators are often guided majorly by three standard-setting bodies; the Basel Committee on Banking Supervision, International Association of Deposit Insurers (IADI) and the Financial Standard Board (FSB). The principles and attributes provided by these bodies in assessing the resolution options from the Nigerian perspective are examined in the remaining parts of the chapter.

Section 11.1 introduces the BCBS-IADI Core Principles for Effective Deposit Insurance Systems (DIS); Section 11.2 presents the FSB Key Attributes of Effective Resolution Regimes and NDIC's level of implementation. Section 11.3 highlights the IADI core principles relevant to failure resolution, Section 11.4 discusses the challenges faced by the NDIC in failure resolution, while Section 11.5 concludes the chapter.

11.1   BCBS-IADI Core Principles for Effective DIS

In June 2009, the Basel Committee on Banking Supervision (BCBS) and IADI jointly issued the Core Principles for Effective Deposit Insurance Systems. These principles laid down important benchmarks for jurisdictions to use in establishing or reforming their DIS. IADI issued a revised set of Core Principles (CPs) and their Compliance Assessment Methodology in November 2014. The CPs were revised downwards from 18 to 16 to reflect the need for effective deposit insurance in preserving financial stability following significant policy lesson from the 2007-09 financial crisis. The evolution of the crisis accentuated the onerous need to safeguard the confidence of depositors in the nation's financial system, which further emphasised the key role that deposit protection plays in achieving that desired confidence (IADI, 2014).

The updated CPs addressed the need for the Deposit Insurer to have additional resolution tools and an ability to be better integrated into the financial safety-net (Nwaigwe, 2017). It is important to note that the revised Core Principles 9, 13, 14 and 15 relate to bank failure resolution and are sources and uses of funding; early detection and timely intervention; failure resolution; and depositors' reimbursement, respectively (see Section 11.3 below for details).

11.2 FSB Key Attributes of Effective Resolution Regimes

The FSB sets out twelve key attributes for effective resolution regimes for financial institutions with the main purpose of identifying core elements considered necessary for an effective resolution regime. It is also aimed at having designated resolution authorities with a broad range of powers to intervene and resolve a non-viable institution. The authorities concerned can allocate losses to shareholders and unsecured/uninsured creditors in their order of seniority. Furthermore, the key attributes allow authorities to manage the failure of large, complex and internationally active financial institutions in a way that minimises severe disruption and avoids recourse to public funds that would expose taxpayers to the risk of loss.

The details of the FSB's key Attributes and the NDIC's level of implementation are as follows:

I. *Scope*
   The resolution regime should be clear and transparent as to the financial institutions within

its scope. The resolution regime should require that at least all domestically incorporated global SIFIs ("G-SIFIs") have in place a recovery and resolution plan.

Also, the 2013 Framework for Supervision of Domestic Systemically Important Banks in Nigeria (D-SIBs) has:

- identified banks that are considered D-SIBs and those that are not; and
- specified the requirement of all D-SIBs to submit their recovery and resolution plans to both CBN and NDIC.

II. *Resolution Authority*

This attributes provides that, each jurisdiction should have a designated administrative authority or authorities, with operational independence, responsible for exercising the resolution powers over banks within the scope of the resolution regime, such that, where there are multiple resolution authorities within a jurisdiction their respective mandates, roles and responsibilities should be clearly defined and coordinated. However, the lead authority should be identified in jurisdictions where different resolution authorities resolve same entities within a single jurisdiction.

Additionally, the resolution authority should have unimpeded access to firms where that is material for the purposes of resolution planning and the preparation and implementation of resolution measures.

In Nigeria, the NDIC and CBN are both the clear resolution authorities with unhindered access to banks both during joint examinations or surveillance. Presently, the status and statistics of all deposit taking financial institutions (DMBs, PMBs and MFBs) are rendered through electronic Financial Analysis Surveillance System (eFASS) to the Central Bank of Nigeria (CBN) and NDIC.

III. Resolution Powers

Resolution authorities should have at their disposal, a broad range of adequate and required resolution powers.

In Nigeria, the NDIC has powers to undertake Open Bank Assistance; Depositor Reimbursement; Purchase and Assumption; Bridge Bank Mechanism; Assisted Mergers and Purchase of Assets, while the CBN has the powers of Open Bank Assistance; Lender of last resort (LOLR). The Asset Management Corporation of Nigeria (AMCON) has powers to purchase NPLs and recapitalise distressed banks. The Ministry of Finance is the guarantor of LOLR.

The NDIC has over the years, garnered experience in the exercise of its resolution powers which have been applied in eight (8) instances as detailed below:

(a) *Open Bank Assistance (OBA)*

Open bank assistance refers to a resolution method in which an insured bank in danger of failing is allowed to continue to operate as a going concern, the deposit insurer intervenes by giving the failing bank some assistance (NDIC, 2009). Some of these include:

i.   Financial Assistance: In accordance with Section 37 (1) of the NDIC Act, NDIC granted Accommodation Facilities amounting to ₦2.3 billion to 10 banks which had serious liquidity problems in 1989.

ii. Imposition of Holding Actions: These were corrective or self-restructuring measures applied to 47 banks as at 1996. Up to 2007, 32 distressed banks had been taken over by the CBN/NDIC to safeguard their assets.

iii. Acquisition & Sale of Banks. CBN/NDIC acquired, restructured and sold seven distressed banks to new investors.

(b) Reimbursement of Depositors of Closed DMBs

Payment of insured deposit is made up to the insurable limit through direct payment and the use of Agent banks. When the failed bank's assets are realised, liquidation dividends are paid to insured depositors on a pro rata basis. Of the forty-nine DMBs whose licences were revoked by the CBN between 1994 and 2006, liquidation activities were on-going in forty-six by the NDIC while the revocation of three remaining licences was being challenged in the court of law by the erstwhile owners. As at 31st December, 2017, the NDIC had paid the sum of ₦8.25 billion to 442,661 insured depositors and liquidation dividends of ₦95.90 billion to 250,497 uninsured depositors of the closed forty-six DMBs. The NDIC in 2013 commenced the use of e-payment and advance payment channels to improve the effectiveness of payment to insured depositors.

(c) Reimbursement of Depositors of Closed PMBs and MFBs

The activities of the NDIC in this regard include the liquidation of one hundred and eighty-seven MFBs and forty-six PMBs whose licences were revoked by the CBN between 2010 and 2014. It is instructive to note that the sum of ₦2.88 billion was paid to 81,611 depositors of the closed MFBs as at December 2017, while ₦68.40 million had been paid to 840 depositors of the closed PMBs as at December 2017.

(d) Purchase and Assumption (P&A)

This is a resolution option in which a healthy bank purchases some or all the assets and assumes some or all the liabilities of the failed bank (NDIC, 2009). Following the completion of the consolidation exercise in December 2005, the number of DMBs decreased from eighty-nine to twenty-five, and thirteen banks that failed to meet the capital requirement of ₦25 billion had their banking licences revoked in January 2006. Section 38(1) of the NDIC Act grants it powers to adopt P&A in resolving banks with problems.

This novel approach was first used in 2006 to resolve the problems of those thirteen banks that failed to either recapitalise or consolidate with other banks. P&A was adopted to give depositors easy access to their funds without condition or disruptions to the banking system, facilitate continuity of banking services in the same premises used by the failed banks, encourage depositors to establish banker-customer relationships with the acquiring bank and promoting banking culture.

(e) Bail out by Government through the CBN

A special audit of twenty-four DMBs by the CBN/ NDIC in June 2009, revealed that banks were afflicted by large volume of non-performing loans, capital erosion, poor risk management and poor corporate governance practices, amongst others. Ten DMBs needed close supervisory monitoring out of which eight were in precarious financial condition. Government injected ₦620 billion into the eight banks as loan capital and liquidity support which had since been recovered by the CBN. CBN mounted a campaign for public confidence by assuring the banking public that no bank would be allowed to fail, and so guaranteed for all the affected banks' interbank takings and foreign credit obligations. As the LOLR, the CBN gives facilities to banks through the Real-Time Gross Settlement system (RTGS) and Deferred Net Settlement system.

(f) Bridge Bank Mechanism

The term refers to a temporary bank established and operated by the deposit insurer to acquire the assets and assume the liabilities of a failed bank until a final resolution is accomplished (NDIC, 2009). When it became clear that the three banks out of the ten found to be in grave financial condition in 2009 could not recapitalise, merge nor find an acquirer on or before September 30, 2011 deadline, bridge bank option was adopted by the NDIC to address their problems as provided in Section 39(1) of NDIC Act, 2006. The bridge bank option was adopted because the three affected banks had attractive franchise and further deterioration in their assets would hamper their sale. Further to that, it would ensure that depositors were protected, thus promoting continuity of banking services to sustain customer confidence. The three bridge banks acquired by AMCON have been successfully sold to private investors.

(g) Assisted Mergers

As part of measures to resolve the problems of four out of the banks identified in 2009 to be in severe financial condition, the regulatory authorities embarked on assisted mergers of the banks in 2011. That effort was further supported by the forbearance provided by government through AMCON and capital injections by the acquiring banks which later brought down the number of DMBs to twenty in 2011 as against twenty-four in 2010.

(h) Purchase of NPLs and Recapitalisation of Distressed Banks

AMCON was established in 2010 by an Act with the mandate to purchase non-performing loans from the banks, recapitalise the technically insolvent banks and enhance availability of credit to the critical sectors of the economy. AMCON acquired the three bridge banks and injected the sum of ₦1.003 trillion into them as capital. They were: Enterprise Bank (₦194.59 billion); Keystone Bank (₦366.89 billion); and Mainstreet Bank (₦451.42. billion). AMCON injected the sum of ₦1.379 trillion into five of the intervened banks (Intercontinental, Oceanic, Finbank, ETB, Union) with a view to facilitating their merger and/or acquisition. NPLs of ₦2.16 trillion was also acquired in twenty banks (including ten troubled banks) at a discounted value of about ₦770.54 billion in FGN backed bonds.

As part of the efforts to meet the resolution cost of restoring financial stability, the Financial Stability Fund (FSF) was set up by CBN in collaboration with the banks in 2010. The CBN was to contribute ₦50 billion annually for ten years while each bank was to contribute 0.3% (later increased to 0.5%) of its total assets annually for ten years. The fund was to ensure that future bank resolution could be achieved with minimum delay and little contribution, if at all, from tax payers' money. It had an initial target of ₦1.5 trillion. In support of that effort, the NDIC reduced the premium burden on banks by decreasing premium base rate from 0.5% (or 50 basis points) to 0.4% (or 40 basis points) and later to 0.35 (or 35 basis points).

IV. Set-off, netting, collateralisation, segregation of client assets

The legal framework governing set-off rights, contractual netting and collateralisation agreements and the segregation of client assets should be clear, transparent and enforceable during a crisis or resolution of firms.

The rule, where applicable, is clear as demonstrated during the 2009 near-banking crisis where the assets of all insured banks were segregated into performing and NPLs.

V. Safeguards

Resolution powers should be exercised in a way that respects the hierarchy of claims. The resolution authority should have the capacity to exercise the resolution powers with the necessary speed and flexibility, subject to constitutionally protected legal remedies and due process.

For NDIC, the depositors have the first right of claims and thereafter, other creditors.

VI. *Funding of Firms in Resolution*

Jurisdictions should have statutory or other policies set in such a way that will not constraint authorities to rely on public ownership or bail out funds as a means of resolving financial crisis of firms. As a last resort and for the overarching purpose of maintaining financial stability, some countries may decide to have power to place the firm under temporary public ownership and control in order to continue critical operations, while seeking to arrange a permanent solution such as sale or merger with a commercial private sector purchaser.

The NDIC, as a well-designed DIS, has in place mechanisms necessary to ensure that adequate funds are available to reimburse depositors promptly in the event of an insured institution's failure and to cover the operating expenses of the system. The NDIC also has in place, a framework on target fund reserve ratio which helps it to determine the adequacy of fund. Funding is mainly through payment of mandatory annual premium as one of the conditions for membership of the DIS. The cumulative premium contributed by insured institutions is called Deposit Insurance Fund (DIF). The NDIC's DIF has grown over the years and stood at ₦959.55 billion as at 31st December, 2017. The law setting up NDIC and subsequent provisions allows the Corporation to introduce special premiums or levies on the participating institutions, when the DIF is not sufficient to resolve some non-systemic failure or borrow from CBN and or federal government, and/or raise bonds guaranteed by the Federal Government when necessary.

VII. *Legal Framework Conditions for Cross-Border Co-operation*

The statutory mandate of a resolution authority should empower and strongly encourage the authority where possible, to act to achieve a cooperative solution with foreign resolution authorities.

This is, however, still under study/consideration in Nigeria. The Corporation, nonetheless, has signed MoUs with a member if deposit insurer across the globe in areas of experience and knowledge sharing in a bid to enhance deposit insurance capacity. Moreso, the MD/CE of the Corporation is currently the Chairman of the IADI African Regional Committee (ARC), a position held since 2018.

VIII. *Crisis Management Groups (CMGs)*

Home and key host authorities of all G-SIFIs should maintain CMGs with the objective of enhancing preparedness for, and facilitating the management and resolution of a cross-border financial crisis affecting the firm.

Nigeria has no institution that is considered to be a G-SIFI, but has Domestic Systemically Important Banks (D-SIBs) with functions that approximate those of the G-SIFI. The Framework for Bank Systemic Crisis has established a Crisis

Management Committee comprising CBN, NDIC, FMF and the Presidency.

IX. *Institution-Specific Cross-Border Co-operation Agreements*
For all G-SIFIs, at a minimum, institution-specific cooperation agreements, containing the essential elements set out in Annex I of the Key Attributes should be in place between the home and relevant host authorities that need to be involved in the planning and crisis resolution stages.

X. *Resolvability Assessments*
Resolution authorities should regularly undertake, at least for G-SIFIs, resolvability assessments that evaluate the feasibility of resolution strategies and their credibility, in light of the likely impact of the firm's failure on the financial system and the overall economy.

As stated earlier, Nigeria has no institution that is considered to be a G-SIFI, but resolvability assessments can be undertaken under the 2013 Framework for Supervision of Domestic SIBs.

XI. *Recovery and Resolution Planning*
Jurisdictions should put in place an ongoing process for recovery and resolution planning, covering at a minimum, domestically incorporated firms that could be systemically significant or critical if they fail.

The 2013 Framework for Supervision of Domestic Systemically Important Banks (D-SIBs) in Nigeria has specified the requirement of all

D-SIBs to submit their resolution plans to both CBN and NDIC.

XII. *Access to Information and Information Sharing*

Jurisdictions should ensure that no legal, regulatory or policy impediments exist that could hinder appropriate exchange of information, including firm-specific information, between supervisory authorities, central banks, resolution authorities, finance ministries and the public authorities responsible for guarantee schemes.

At present, CBN, NDIC and other regulators have full access to data and information of all regulated firms. There is no impediment to data access by regulators. The FSRCC ensures seamless information sharing and access by all Nigerian regulators.

Table 11.11

Bank Failure and Extent of Failure in Nigeria 1994–2006

Year of Closure	No of Banks	Total Assets (N'B)	Total Deposits (N'B)	Ratio of Assets Close of Banks to Total Assets of Banks Ind (%)	Ratio of Assets of Close Banks to Total Deposits of Banks Ind (%)	Ratio of Assets of Close Banks to GDP (%)	Number of Depositors
1994	4	6.10	2.00	1.94	1.12	0.66	6,411
1995	1	0.40	0.80	0.09	0.38	0.02	7,416
1998	26	34.60	16.30	4.50	4.34	1.11	1,709,343
2000	3	2.70	3.80	0.14	0.45	0.06	31,969
2002	1	20.20	11.60	0.68	0.95	0.35	228,585
2003	1	2.10	3.41	0.06	0.24	0.03	1,044
2006	13	160.10	177.28	1.23	4.69	0.55	961,211
TOTAL	49	165.9	215.19	0.93	2.59	0.44	3,165,979

Source: NDIC Annual Report, 1994–2006

11.3 IADI Core Principles

The Core Principles for Effective Deposit Insurance Systems sets important benchmark for jurisdictions to use in establishing or reforming deposit insurance systems. The Core Principles, published on 18th June, 2009, were designed by the Basel Committee on Banking Supervision (BCBS) and the International Association of Deposit Insurers (IADI) to address a comprehensive range of issues including coverage, funding, powers, membership, transitioning from blanket to limited coverage and prompt reimbursement.

A Steering Committee established by IADI in February 2013 was mandated to undertake a revision of the Core Principles and their recommendations for a revision of the principles from 18 to 16, which was formally published in November 2014. The revised Core Principles strengthen the deposit insurance standards in several areas including reimbursement speed, coverage, funding and governance, adding more guidance on the deposit insurer's role in crisis preparedness and management (IADI, 2020). Below are the revised core principles.

1. Public Policy Objectives
2. Mandate and Powers
3. Governance
4. Relationships with Other Safety-Net Participants
5. Cross-Border Issues
6. Deposit Insurer's Role in Contingency Planning and Crisis Management
7. Membership
8. Coverage
9. Sources and Uses of Fund
10. Public Awareness

11. Legal Protection
12. Dealing with Parties at Fault in a Bank Failure
13. Early Detection and Timely Intervention
14. Failure Resolution
15. Reimbursing Depositors
16. Recoveries

Below are the BCBS-IADI core principles for effective deposit insurance systems that are relevant to bank failure resolution:

i) **Core Principle 9**
    Sources and uses of funding: This core principle stresses industry as source of funding, and the need for wide range of ex ante or ex-post tools so as to ensure prompt reimbursement in times of failure.

ii) **Core Principle 13**
    Early detection and timely intervention: This requires that the deposit insurer should be part of a framework within the financial system safety-net that provides for the early detection and timely intervention and resolution of troubled banks. This is especially the case in instances of risk minimiser mandate, such as is obtainable in Nigeria.

iii) **Core Principle 14**
    Failure resolution: This seeks to ensure that the deposit insurer is able to reimburse depositors promptly and minimise resolution costs and disruption of markets. Also, deposit insurers or other relevant financial system safety-net participants should have the authority to establish a bridge institution should the need arise.

iv) *Core Principle 15*

Reimbursing depositors: This states that the deposit insurance system should reimburse the depositors' insured fund promptly in order to contribute to financial stability. There should therefore be a clear and unequivocal trigger for insured depositor reimbursement.

11.4 Challenges

As should be expected, the NDIC has in the course of discharging its mandate encountered some challenges. The challenges include the following:

i) Cumbersome, slow and bureaucratic judicial process resulting in long-drawn out litigation on winding-up actions and debt recovery matters.

ii) Poor public awareness.

iii) Uncooperative attitude toward the bank closing team.

iv) Poor record keeping (financial, mandate records, broken down IT systems, etc.).

v) Problems of asset realisation (loans and physical assets) due to large size of insider loans, poor loan documentation, poor quality, lack of secondary market and court sympathy for debtors and weak title for landed properties.

vi) Issues relating to planning and coordination of parties that are involved in the establishment of bridge bank, SEC, CAC, CBN, AMCON, FMF, etc.

vii) The confidentiality requirement for the establishment of a bridge bank.

viii) Court action by erstwhile shareholders.

11.5 Conclusion

This chapter has shown the Nigerian experience in bank resolution and measures adopted over the years and how the NDIC has carried out its role in that regard. Deposit insurance system is designed to protect depositors (especially small depositors/savers) and thus promote confidence. The NDIC experience has been a rewarding one through the discharge of its core mandate and responsibility over the years. NDIC will continue to research into and evaluate the suitability of relevant new tool kits as they emerge.

References

Adeleke, A. A. (2015). Bank Failure Resolution Measures: Experience in Nigeria. An NDIC Presentation

Afolabi, J. A. (2014). Bank Failure Resolution Measures: Experiences in Nigeria. An NDIC Presentation

Anyadeigwu, A. E. (2017). Effective Resolution Regimes. (Framework, Resolution Options, Key Features, Challenges and Milestones) Being a paper presented at the IADI, Africa Regional Committee/Middle East North Africa Technical Assistance Workshop. Casablanca Morocco. 27th -30th March 2017

Eisenbeis, R. A. and Kaufman, G. G. (2010). Deposit Insurance. In: Berger, A. N. Molyneux, P. and Wilson, J. O. S. (eds). 2010. *The Oxford Handbook of Banking.* Oxford: Oxford University Press. pp.339-356

Financial Stability Forum (2001). Guidance for Developing Effective Deposit Insurance System

FSB (2014). Key Attributes of Effective Resolution Regimes for Financial Institutions, 15 October, 2014

IADI (2014). IADI Core Principles for Effective Deposit Insurance System, November 2014

Ibrahim, U. (2017). IADI Core Principles for effective Deposit Insurance Scheme Being a paper presented at the Conference on Resolution and Deposit Insurance, Cape town, South Africa

Kyei, A. (1995). 'Deposit Protection Arrangements: A Survey', *IMF Working Paper* 95/134 Washington

Nwaigwe, K. O. (2017). BCBS-IADI Core Principles for Effective Deposit Insurance Systems. Being a presentation at the NDIC Academy on Fundamentals of DIS

Nigeria Deposit Insurance Corporation, NDIC (2009). 20 years of Deposit Insurance in Nigeria

12

BUILDING BLOCKS TO SUSTAINABLE BANKING PRACTICE IN NIGERIA[11]

12.0 Introduction

One way in which corporate entities have contributed to environmental conservation in recent years is through the promotion of sustainable practices in their activities. In recent times, the promotion of a clean environment through improved banking practices, known as "Sustainable Banking" has become prominent.

The journey towards embracing sustainable banking practice in Nigeria formally commenced with the release of a written declaration on it by the Bankers' Committee in October 2011. The declaration states:

> The Banker subcommittee on economic development and sustainability in conjunction with sector regulators and financial services providers, hereby commits to the following set of principles known as the Nigerian

11 Original version of this paper was presented at the Regional Consultative Group Sub-Sahara Workshop on Recovery and Resolution Planning held in Ghana, May 6-9, 2014.

sustainable banking principles (Bankers' Committee Retreat, 2012).

The Committee pledged to adopt the principles in recognition of the Nigerian banking sector's role and responsibility to deliver positive development that impact on the society, whilst protecting the communities and environments in which the banks operate.

Subsequent to the work that followed the declaration of commitment, the Central Bank of Nigeria (CBN), on September 24, 2012, passed a circular on the implementation of Sustainable Banking Principles by Banks, Discount Houses and Development Finance Institutions in Nigeria. Issues covered therein included highlights of the nine sustainable banking principles and their contextualisation to fit the Nigerian environment; guidance notes to the principles; and sector guidelines that covered the three sectors, namely: power, agriculture and oil and gas; as well as the related laws and regulations that govern their operations. The document as well as the decision to adopt it as a policy, represented a significant development and indeed, a watershed in the history of banking in Nigeria.

The purpose of this chapter is to provide further insights into the building blocks for sustainable banking practice in Nigeria. For ease of appreciation, the rest of the chapter is organised into six sections. Section 12.1 provides a review of the concept of sustainable banking practice. A discussion on sustainable banking practice in Nigeria, including the development of the nine cardinal principles of sustainable banking is covered in Section 12.2. Section 12.3 discusses the major building blocks to sustainable banking practice in Nigeria, including the roles of regulatory authorities toward the implementation of the principles. In Section 12.4, some of the initiatives of CBN and NDIC are highlighted. Section 12.5 examines implementation challenges for sustainable banking in Nigeria and Section 12.6 concludes the chapter.

12.1 The Concept of Sustainable Banking Practice

Sustainable banking is an approach that recognises the role of banks in driving long-term economic development that is not only economically viable but also environmentally responsible and socially relevant (CBN, 2012). It can also be viewed as a value system which ensures that the activities of banks do not only benefit its staff, shareholders, customers and the economy, but also minimises any unintended negative effects on the society and the natural environment.

The practice of sustainable banking, with a moral tone, has been in existence since the 16th century, with Italian banks operating on moral ethics, such as avoidance of usury and community-support for financing local businesses (Weber, 2012). This practice metamorphosed into Credit Unions and Cooperative Banks, addressing the need of financial services for the new middle-class and entrepreneurs. Over time, the practice of community finance or local business fizzled out, as transnational banks started to control the global financial industry and began to create financial products that did not support the real economy and did not take into account the socio-economic and environmental impact of the communities in which they operated. In the 1980s, a regulation of liabilities on contaminated sites was introduced in the Americas. Similar regulations with respect to soil, water and air pollution were introduced in Europe at that time. That changed the relationship between the financial sector and the environment significantly. In cases which lenders had used sites as collateral, the value of the collateral could be diminished by contaminations and clean-up costs for which lenders were held liable. According to Weber (2012), in order to mitigate these risks, lenders started to integrate environmental issues into credit risk.

Sustainable banking by conventional financial institutions was heralded with the management of environmental risks that negatively affected the financial institutions, especially with regard to credit risk. After this phase of risk management, the financial sector took the business opportunities offered by integrating environmental and social issues into consideration. Sustainability therefore became a business case in the financial sector, as financial institutions explored ways to influence sustainable development in a positive way. They developed products and services taking sustainability issues into account. Green loan originations (e.g. low-carbon credit cards, green bonds, carbon finance, etc.) and screening and managing environmental and social risks as part of bank's decision-making processes were adopted by leading international banks.

Some achievements have also been recorded by banks practising sustainable banking. For instance, green loan borrowers in China increased by 86% within one year and green lending balance reached US$62 billion in 2015. In addition, green loan lending accounted for about 16% of total banking sector lending in 2015, and is still growing rapidly. In China, it is estimated that energy-saving emission reduction is equivalent to the total amount of carbon dioxide absorbed by forests each year totalling 7.16 million hectares (IFC, 2018[12]).

Sustainability from regulatory and management perspectives cover both corporate governance and risk management failures which, as emphasised in a couple of chapters above, could expose customers to great financial risks, harming communities and the environment. Such negative impacts might not only damage a bank's commercial image as the immediate consequence, but also suffer reputational damage that could impair its long-term sustainability (SAS, 2013). Regulatory and reputational risk management are two sides of the same coin such that if the bank fails in one, it fails in the other.

Environmental and social risks of lending could be high and that explains why banks need to develop environmental and social risk management (ESRM) policies through the establishments of dedicated units to assess the risks and advise on appropriate mitigants, including, if necessary, rejecting certain deals (SAS, 2013). Banks should also commission special audit and assure firms to provide independent verification of their sustainability reporting. Sustainability audit improves the overall risk of management and business performance. The Dutch financial conglomerate, ING, in one of its corporate social responsibility reports recommended "that acting responsibly results in better and more comprehensive risk management, a higher degree of employee pride, a greater attraction (of the bank) for talented people and new business opportunities" (SAS, 2013).

---

12   https://www.ifc.org/wps/wcm/connect/accessed August 2018.

12.2 Sustainable Banking Practice in Nigeria

In 2011, the Nigerian banking community through its Bankers' Committee committed to adopting sustainable banking practice. The commitment was based on their understanding that such an approach was consistent with their individual and collective business objectives and business opportunities. And that it would promote more investments to stimulate further economic growth and enhance innovation and competitiveness.

To facilitate the introduction of the practice, the Bankers' Committee assigned the responsibility for the development of the sustainability principles and sector guidelines to its sub-committee on Economic Development, which in turn set up a Strategic Sustainable Workgroup (SSWG), made up of members from the Banks, Discount Houses, CBN, NDIC, Federal Ministry of Environment, Nigeria Electricity Regulatory Commission, National Energy Commission, International Finance Corporation (IFC), the Netherlands Development Finance Company (FMO), Federal Ministry of Water Resources and Federal Ministry of Agriculture. Each of these members equally constituted the Sustainability Champions in their organisations. The workgroup and sustainability champion came up with the "Nigeria Sustainable Banking Principles" (NSBP) and guidelines for the three chosen sectors of the economy, namely: agriculture, oil & gas and power. The choice of the three sectors was informed by the fact that they constituted the critical sectors that drive the Nigerian economy and the fact that banks in Nigeria are more exposed to at least, two of these sectors while government placed high priority on agriculture.

The NSBP, based on leading international sustainable finance standards and established industry best practice (CBN, 2012), are:

1. Managing environmental and social risk in business decisions;
2. Managing the bank's own environmental and social footprint;
3. Safeguarding human rights;
4. Promoting women's economic participation/ empowerment;
5. Promoting financial inclusion of communities and groups with limited or no access to the formal financial sector;
6. Meeting the imperatives for good governance, transparency and accountability;
7. Supporting capacity building in the sector;
8. Promoting collaborative partnerships that will accelerate sector progress; and
9. Reporting to take stock of sector progress and attendant needs.

The NSBP requires each bank to develop an Environment and Social Risks (E&S) management system, which incorporates the principles and balances, the identification of E&S risk and the opportunities (CBN, 2012). The degree and level of E&S management should commensurate with the scale and scope of a bank's business activities and operations. Each bank will also apply the principles to its domestic operations.

In addition, banks were expected to develop and submit to the CBN, an overarching sustainable banking commitment, which articulates how they will apply the principles and guidelines, how E&S risk management considerations have been integrated into the enterprise risk management framework and their implementation targets and milestones, including a five-year plan. Furthermore, they were required to make regular submissions regarding the implementation and compliance with the principles and guidelines to their Board of Directors and regulatory authorities; engage their respective Board of Directors on the principles and guidelines; designate a sustainable banking desk or unit responsible for implementation and begin capacity building with relevant stakeholders, amongst other responsibilities.

The CBN directed full adoption and implementation of these principles by all members of the Bankers' Committee. It also currently supports them by providing incentives to those institutions that take concrete measures to incorporate the provisions of these principles and guidelines into their operational enterprise risk management and other governance frameworks.

The adoption of the principles and guidelines by the relevant institutions in Nigeria, signify the integration of social and environmental considerations into their operations, policies, processes, procedures, as well as provision of structural mechanism to support implementation at the industry level. The responsibility lay with banks to interpret and apply these principles to their core values, business model and enterprise risk management framework.

The advent of sustainable banking among Nigerian banks increased their corporate social responsibility function and ensured that banking was carried out in a manner that will preserve the environment.

12.3   Building Blocks to Sustainable Banking Practice in Nigeria

Virtually everything contained in the document on sustainable banking practice in Nigeria was critical and needed to be holistically appreciated and implemented, taking into account individual banks' circumstances. However, the following are some extracts considered very crucial to Nigeria's journey to evolve sustainable banking practice in the country.

12.3.1   *Leadership Commitment*

The starting point in the journey to a sustainable banking culture was the expression of leadership commitment. Introducing sustainable banking practices in a bank was certainly a major organisational change, failure of which could have costly results on the bank, including putting the very future of the organisation at risk. Management literature reveal that effective change management must be spearheaded by senior management who should have full commitment and comprehensive awareness of the different roles and capabilities at all levels of the organisation (Schroeder-Saulnier, 2009). They must also be able to define and measure success and periodically assess progress. Structurally, therefore, leadership commitment should begin from the topmost level and cascade down to various leadership levels in the organisation. The commitment should not only be internalised, but should find expression in policies and decisions to be made, which should facilitate implementation of the principles.

12.3.2 Policy Framework

A robust policy framework must be developed to define the bank's commitment and approach to sustainable banking and implementation of the principles. The framework should include:

12.3.2.1 Modalities of Application

Clear articulation should be made on how the principles will be relevant to various activities and operations of the banks and how they can be applied without creating dislocations. Justifying the relevance and how they will be applied should no doubt facilitate understanding and buy-in as well as continuous commitment of the various internal stakeholders.

12.3.2.2 Review of Decision-Making Processes

The new dispensation will necessitate a review of the decision-making processes of the bank to allow appropriate integration of the sustainable banking principles into existing internal processes, where applicable, a bank's enterprise risk management framework. The new system should provide assessment criteria and decision framework that accommodates E&S management system.

12.3.2.3 Application of Relevant International E&S Standards and Industry Best Practice

In addition to compliance with local laws, all banks shall apply, where relevant, international E&S standards and industry best practice such as the International Finance Corporation (IFC) Performance Standards, the

Equator Principles for project finance, the World Bank Group Environmental Health and Safety Guidelines for lending to different sector activities. For instance, the IFC performance standards, which are directed towards clients, provide guidance on how to identify risks and impacts, and are also designed to help avoid, mitigate, and manage risks and impacts as a way of doing business in a sustainable way. They also include stakeholder engagement and disclosure obligations of the client in relation to project activities (IFC, 2012). Similarly, Equator Principles[13] are recognised risk management framework, adopted by financial institutions for determining, assessing and managing environmental and social risks in projects, primarily intended to provide a minimum standard for due diligence to support responsible risk decision-making.

12.3.2.4 Establishment of Clear Governance Structures

The governance structures should clearly address the new business direction, which considers environmental and social (E&S) issues. Governance and its structures have been clearly recognised to determine success or failure of establishments. Thus, roles and responsibilities, practices and standards, codes of conduct, performance-linked incentives, audit procedures and disclosure requirements must be clearly spelt out. In the new dispensation, client disclosure obligations must include, where necessary, environmental and social impact assessment.

---

13   www.equator-principles.com/index.

12.3.2.5   Capacity-Building Requirements

As a bank signed up to the challenge of sustainable banking, it should correspondingly brace up to the challenge of capacity building. Capacity building is essential for the industry to successfully attain the benefits sustainable banking promises to offer not just to the industry, but also to the larger society. The implementation of the NSBP involves a complex interplay between economic, environmental and socio-cultural considerations, which will require innovative thinking, new approaches, and, very fundamentally, the capacity to implement them. Capacity building in this context should be holistic, encompassing a number of activities that include building abilities, relationships and values that will enable the banks, individually and collectively, to improve their performance and achieve the objectives of sustainable banking. There will be need to engender willingness on the part of staff to play new developmental roles; strengthen the legal infrastructure and other processes and systems; develop new institutional mechanisms; and deploy new and appropriate technologies to facilitate implementation.

By implication therefore, capacity building should be central to sustainable banking agenda and should focus on acquisition of up-to-date information, knowledge, tools and skills to address various issues without ignoring or sacrificing the main banking functions and services. A bank will be expected to provide the necessary resources and support to equip and train employees on E&S management approaches based on roles, responsibilities and functions. Indeed, as part of its sustainable banking policy and E&S management system, a bank should develop a sector-specific E&S approach and competencies for the three priority sectors of power, agriculture and oil and gas in order to fast track its implementation. It is important to note that developing competencies that would ensure the success of sustainable banking practices must cover top levels of management as well as all relevant employees in the organisation, and this will have to be on a continuous basis.

12.3.2.6   *Stakeholder Collaboration*

Stakeholder cooperation is very critical in organisational game of survival, continuity and success. Stakeholders include owners of businesses and their customers, competitors, employees, suppliers, governments, local community organisations, special interest groups, environmentalists, consumer advocates, media, unions, trade associations, financial community and political groups. The stakeholder cooperation therefore underscores the need for collective efforts, in varying degrees and at various levels, to ensure survival and sustainability of the organisation. Thus, for sustainable banking in Nigeria to take root, it must involve the participation of all key stakeholders who should recognise the need for interdependence and synergy in their respective roles. Such collaboration should find expression in four basic value considerations, namely:

i.   Transparency (full disclosure of financial and non-financial information);

ii. Accountability (ensuring that management is effectively overseen by competent governing body);

iii. Fairness (equitable treatment of clients in line with the provisions of sustainable banking principles); and

iv. Responsibility (ensuring banks fulfil their proper roles in society).

12.3.2.7   *Self-Regulation*

Self-regulation is a system where an institution or an association to which an institution belongs, imposes on itself, certain standards that facilitate the achievement of its objectives within the framework of existing legislative provisions. Self-regulation is no doubt one of the foremost factors in achieving organisational discipline and, of course, organisational sustainability. It facilitates effective monitoring and modification of behaviour to attain a given goal. It also gives room for responsible service, engenders consumer trust, increases patronage and allows healthy competition. The strength of self-regulation is anchored on the fact that managers see the organisations as their pets, which they should nurture and protect whether or not external regulators and supervisors keep watch.

Sustainability therefore, will require banking institutions to go extra miles in the areas of self-regulation and self-assessment, which can be achieved through additional dedication, patience and internal consensus.

12.3.2.8   *Legislative/Regulatory Imperative*

Despite the relevance and, in fact, desirability of self-regulation, the nature and limitations of individuals who run organisations have always necessitated the need for legislations and regulations to protect public interest and foster welfare and economic development. Thus, although self-regulation is highly canvassed, it is not an alternative to government statutory regulation and its effective deployment. Effective regulation requires inputs from industry associations, international bodies, non-governmental organisations and community groups as well as involves mechanisms ranging from rules, codes, monitoring and sanctions. The success of sustainable banking in Nigeria will therefore also be hinged significantly on the extent to which regulatory agencies carry out their supervisory and oversight functions on various aspects of banking services. This will require development and/or enhancement of appropriate supervisory capacity on the part of the regulators. Efforts should therefore be intensified to adopt risk-based and consolidated supervision and prompt corrective actions as may be necessary. However, because sustainable banking goes beyond simple relationship between banks and their clients, to include social and environmental concerns, other institutional stakeholders should see the development or enhancement of their respective sector regulations and their effective deployment as a matter of great importance to facilitate sustainable banking in the country.

12.3.2.9 Measuring and Reporting Implementation Progress

In order to keep track of their performance, banks would be expected to articulate objectives, performance indicators and milestones. Performance tracking enables a bank to measure its progress in implementing the principles as well as its sustainable banking policies and procedures. As part of its public commitment to adopting the principles, it is required that a bank reports publicly its implementation progress on an annual basis. Specifically, after a bank has established appropriate sustainable banking commitment and implementation plan, it is expected to develop a reporting template that:

(a) is consistent with the objectives and reporting requirements of each principle; and

(b) aligned with the core values and business model of the bank.

12.4 Initiatives of CBN and NDIC in Promoting Sustainable Banking

Both the CBN and NDIC, as members of the Bankers' Committee, pledged their commitment to the adoption and implementation of the NSBP. For that reason, they are under the obligation to lead by example. In 2012, for example, the CBN joined the membership of the Sustainable Banking Network (SBN) launched by the International Finance Corporation (IFC). Members of the SBN have uniform interest in policies, guidelines and initiatives that support the financial sector to adopt environmental and social risk management and green lending. In addition, the CBN as part of the initiatives (Mahmood, 2013) for implementing the principles, has:

a) Developed a sustainability implementation plan;

b) Set up a sustainability committee to drive the implementation of the principles in the bank;

c) Commenced training of staff members of the CBN sustainability committee;

d) Sensitised departmental heads and branch controllers on sustainable banking; and

e) Raised awareness of employees on sustainability via intranet/bank net.

The NDIC, on its part, to facilitate the implementation of the principles through its operations has:

i. Obtained Board buy-in for the implementation of NSBP.

ii. Placed sensitisation of Board on NSBP as a continuous exercise, especially during the NDIC Board Retreats.

iii. Set up sustainability desk in the Managing Director's office.

iv. Appointed a coordinator to oversee the implementation of the NSBP in the Corporation.

v. Set up a committee on sustainability to facilitate the implementation of NSBP in the Corporation.

vi. Organised awareness sessions on sustainable banking for the staff of the Corporation in Abuja and Lagos.

vii. Hired an expert on sustainability for in-depth training programmes for staff of the Corporation.

With regards to the adoption and implementation of NSBP by the banking industry players, the CBN and NDIC have the responsibility for ensuring that members of Bankers' Committee complied with the requirements of the sustainability principles. In that regard, the CBN, came up with the following initiatives (Mahmood, 2013):

i. Developed a reporting template, which had been exposed to the department dealing with the returns from the industry.

ii. Engaged government MDAs such as Ministry of Environment, Nigeria Security Printing and Minting Plc, etc.

iii. Discussed with Development Finance Institutions (DFIs) such as International Finance Corporation (IFC) and the Netherlands Development Finance Company, for training programmes to build institutional capacity of the industry.

iv. Discussed with the local training institutions such as Financial Institutions Training Centre (FITC), Chartered Institute of Bankers of Nigeria (CIBN) and Lagos Business School, for customised training for the industry.

The NDIC, came up with the following initiatives toward ensuring that the banking industry implements the sustainable banking principles:

a) Made input into the reporting template developed by the CBN.

b) Engaged a consultant in running capacity building programmes for the NDIC examiners who would ensure compliance by the industry.

12.5 Challenges of NSBP Implementation

Some of the challenges encountered in the course of implementing the NSBP include, but not limited to:

i. *Dearth of Capacity:* There is need for capacity building by both the regulators and operators in such areas as identification, assessment and management of E&S risks; E&S cost-benefit analysis; integration of sustainability criteria in operations, etc.

ii. *Compliance and Enforcement:* Regulators should put in place an enabling operating environment for operators, including incentives for compliance. Regulators should also apply sanctions on defaulting institutions as a means of ensuring strict compliance.

iii. *Public Awareness:* Since sustainable banking is novel in our jurisdiction, there is the challenge of having to educate both the staff of banks and the banking public on the new approach to banking practice. This will go a long way in facilitating the implementation of the principles in the system.

12.6 Conclusion

Rising global environmental challenges and their hazardous impact on the welfare of citizenry require that proactive steps be taken to address environmental sustainability issues. In the face of other competing demands, it is obvious that government cannot singlehandedly solve the problem without the support of other stakeholders in the system. There is therefore the need for various stakeholders to sustain the "Sustainable Banking" thrust. With a massive level of buy-in, by the relevant and critical financial institutions in the country, there is no doubt that the implementation of sustainable banking practice can be upheld in Nigeria. What is needed is the sustenance of that commitment, which is crucial to the realisation of the goals of sustainable banking in Nigeria.

References

Bankers' Committee Retreat (2012). "Nigerian Sustainable Banking Principle". Final Version. www.cbn. gov.ng/out/2012/ccd/circular-nsbp-pdf

CBN (2012). "The Nigerian Sustainable Banking Principles. Guidance Note. Implementation of Sustainable Banking Principles by Banks, Discount Houses and Development Finance Institutions in Nigeria. Circular No. *FPR/DIR/CIR/GEN/01/33*.https://www.cbn.gov.ng/out/2012/ccd/circular-nsbp.pdf

Croitoru, L. and Sarraf, M. (2010). "The Cost of Environmental Degradation: Case Studies from the Middle East and North Africa. Edited by Croitoru, L. and Sarraf, M. ISBN: 978-0-8213-8318-6, The World Bank

IFC (2012). International Finance Corporation Performance Standards on Environmental and Social Sustainability, January 2012

Kuhlman, T. and Farrington, J. (2010). "What is Sustainability?" *Sustainability* 2010, 2, pp. 3436-3448. ISSN 2071-1050

Mahmood, A. U. (2013). "Update on Implementation of Nigerian Sustainable Banking", Paper presented at the Sensitization Programme for NDIC staff

Sarraf, M., Larsen, B. and Owaygen, M. (2004). "Cost of Environmental Degradation- The Case of Lebanon and Tunisia. Environmental Economics Series Paper No. 97. The World Bank

SAS (2013). "White Paper on Sustainable Banking", ww.sas. com/reg/wp/24356

Schroeder-Saulnier, D. (2009). Responding to Change Agility: The Leader's Role, Right Management. www. equator-principles.com/index

Weber, O. (2012). "Sustainable Banking-History and Current Developments". Available at SSRN: https://ssrn. com/abstract=2159947 or http://dx.doi.org/10.2139/ ssrn.2159947. Working Paper, School of Environment, Enterprise and Development (SEED), University of Waterloo, ON

INDEX

Printed in the United States
by Baker & Taylor Publisher Services

Printed in the United States
by Baker & Taylor Publisher Services